OTHERWISE ENGAGED
and other plays

First seen at the Queen's Theatre in July 1975 in a
production directed by Harold Pinter, *Otherwise
Engaged* is Simon Gray's first stage play since the
enormously successful *Butley*. With his wife away,
Simon Hench, successful publisher and avid Wagnerite,
is looking forward to a long, luxurious listen to his
brand new record of Parsifal. But the sex problems
of his unprepossessing lodger and his brother's desire
to share his anxiety over his prospects for an Assistant
Headmastership turn out to be just the beginning of a
string of interruptions which increasingly draw
Simon himself into a vicious vortex of accusations
and recriminations.

The London production opened to a unanimously
favourable critical reception:
'Simon Gray's *Otherwise Engaged* is incomparably
his best play to date: adult and literate, scathingly
funny but ultimately disturbing.'
> Frank Marcus, *Sunday Telegraph*

'. . . excellence that dazzles . . .'
> Milton Shulman, *Evening Standard*

'*Otherwise Engaged* is not the kindest play in London;
but it is the most entertaining and the most brilliant.'
> Harold Hobson, *Sunday Times*

In the same volume are two new television plays
by Simon Gray, *Two Sundays* and *Plaintiffs and
Defendants*, first screened on BBC-TV in October
1975. These are thematically related not only to
each other but also to *Otherwise Engaged*. Together
they afford a unique example of the author's ability
to shape his material to the different requirements
of stage and television.

by the same author

Plays

Sleeping Dog (published by Faber)
Wise Child (published by Faber)
Dutch Uncle (published by Faber)
Spoiled (published by Eyre Methuen)
The Idiot (published by Eyre Methuen)
Butley (published by Eyre Methuen)
Dog Days (published by Eyre Methuen)

Novels

Colmain (published by Faber)
Little Portia (published by Faber)
Simple People (published by Faber)
A Comeback for Stark (under the pseudonym
Hamish Reade, published by Faber)

Simon Gray

OTHERWISE ENGAGED
and other plays

EYRE METHUEN · LONDON

First published in 1975 by Eyre Methuen Ltd
11 New Fetter Lane, London EC4P 4EE
Reprinted 1977
Copyright © 1975 by Simon Gray
Printed in Great Britain by
Whitstable Litho Ltd, Whitstable, Kent

ISBN 0 413 34420 7 (Hardback)
ISBN 0 413 34430 4 (Paperback)

The photographs on the front cover show (top) Ian Charleson and Alan Bates in a scene from the Queen's Theatre production of Otherwise Engaged *(photograph reproduced by courtesy of Donald Cooper); Alan Bates in the BBC-TV production of* Plaintiffs and Defendants *(bottom left); and (bottom right) Alan Bates and Dinsdale Landen in* Two Sundays *(photographs reproduced by courtesy of the BBC). The photograph on the back cover is reproduced by courtesy of Beryl Gray.*

CONTENTS

For Harold
Two summers 1971 and 1975

OTHERWISE
ENGAGED

OTHERWISE ENGAGED was first presented on 30th July 1975, at the Queen's Theatre by Michael Codron with the following cast:

SIMON	Alan Bates
DAVE	Ian Charleson
STEPHEN	Nigel Hawthorne
JEFF	Julian Glover
DAVINA	Jacqueline Pearce
WOOD	Benjamin Whitrow
BETH	Mary Miller

Directed by Harold Pinter

Act One

The living-room of the HENCH's *house in London. It is both elegant and comfortable, but not large. Two sofas, two armchairs, a coffee table, a telephone with an answering machine, an extremely expensive and elaborate hi-fi set, and around the walls shelves to accommodate a great range of books (which are evidently cherished) and an extensive collection of records, in which Wagner and other opera sets can be distinguished.*

Stage left is a door that leads onto a small hall, at one end of which is the front door, and at the other a door which, in its turn, when opened reveals a passage that goes onto stairs going down to the basement. More stairs lead up from the hall to another section of the house. The house has, in fact, recently been divided into two, so that there is a top flat.

Stage right has a door that leads to the kitchen, and as becomes evident, there is a door that opens from the kitchen into the garden.

When the curtain goes up, SIMON *is unwrapping a new record. He takes it out with the air of a man who is deeply looking forward to listening to it - there are several records, in fact - the complete Parsifal. He goes to the hi-fi, puts the first record on, listens, adjusts the level, then goes to the sofa and settles himself in it. The opening chords of Parsifal fill the theatre.*

The door opens, left. DAVE *enters.* SIMON *turns, looks at him, concealing his irritation as* DAVE *wanders into the kitchen, returns, and sits restlessly in the armchair. A pause in the music.*

DAVE. What's that then?

   SIMON *gets up and switches off the record.*

SIMON. Wagner. Do you like him?

DAVE (*standing up*). No, well I mean he was anti-semitic, wasn't he. Sort of early fascist, ego-manic type.

SIMON. What about his music, do you like that?

DAVE. Well, I mean, I'm not likely to like his music if I don't like his type, am I?

SIMON (*concealing his impatience*). Everything all right? In the flat, that is. No complaints or other urgencies?

DAVE. No, no, that's all right. Oh, you mean about the rent?

SIMON. Good God no, I wasn't thinking about the rent.

DAVE. It's all right if it waits a bit then, is it?

SIMON. Good God yes, pay us this week's when you pay us last week's - next week, or whenever.

DAVE. OK I'm a bit short, you know how it is. Your wife out again then?

SIMON. Yes, she's gone to (*Thinks.*) Salisbury. She left last night.

DAVE. That girl in the first year came round last night for something to eat. I dropped down to borrow a chop or something, fish fingers would have done.

SIMON. Would they really?

DAVE. But she wasn't here, your wife.

SIMON. No, she wouldn't have been, as she was either in or on her way to Salisbury.

DAVE. So I had to take her out for a kebab and some wine. Then I had to get her to come back.

SIMON. Ah, she stayed the night then? Good for you!

DAVE. No, she didn't.

SIMON. Oh. You managed to get rid of her, then, instead, well done!

DAVE. She just left by herself.

SIMON. Before you had a chance to get rid of her, oh dear, why?

DAVE. Said she didn't fancy me.

SIMON. Good God, why ever not?

DAVE. I don't know. I mean I asked her if she'd like a screw and she said no. Then I asked her why not, and she said she didn't fancy me, that was why not.

SIMON. Still, she's left the door open for a platonic relationship.

DAVE. Yeah, well, then she went off to see something on television with some friend. I haven't got a television.

SIMON. Well, I'm afraid I can't help you there, nor have we.

DAVE. Anyway she said she might be going to that Marxist bookshop down the road today.

SIMON. What time?

DAVE. About lunch time, she said.

SIMON. But good God, lunch will soon be on you, hadn't you better get going - it would be tragic to miss her.

DAVE. Yeah, well that's it, you see. I'm a bit short, like I said. I mean we can't do anything -

Pause.

SIMON. Can I lend you some?

DAVE. What?

SIMON. Can I lend you some money?

DAVE. Yeah, OK.

SIMON (*giving him a fiver*). Is that enough?

DAVE. Yeah. Right. (*Takes it.*) That's five.

SIMON. Well, I'll get back to my music while you're making your own.

STEPHEN (*enters, through the kitchen door*). Hello. Oh hello.

SIMON (*concealing his dismay*). Oh, Stephen. This is Dave, who's taken over the upstairs flat. Dave, my brother Stephen.

STEPHEN. Oh yes, you're at the Poly, aren't you?

DAVE. That's right.

STEPHEN. What are you studying?

DAVE. Sociology.

STEPHEN. That must be jolly interesting. What aspect?

DAVE. What?

STEPHEN. Of sociology.

DAVE. Oh, the usual stuff.

STEPHEN. Psychology, statistics, politics, philosophy, I suppose.

DAVE. We're sitting in at the moment.

STEPHEN. Really? Why?

DAVE. Oh, usual sort of thing. Well - (*Goes towards the door and out.*)

STEPHEN: What is the usual thing?

SIMON. No idea.

STEPHEN (*after a pause*). Well, I must say!

SIMON. Oh, he's not as thick as he seems.

STEPHEN. Isn't he? He certainly seems quite thick. (*Sits down.*) I'm surprised a student could afford that flat, what do you charge him?

SIMON. Two pounds a week, I think.

STEPHEN. But you could get, good Heavens, even through the rent tribunal, ten times that.

SIMON. Oh, we're not out to make money from it.

STEPHEN. Well, *he* seems rather an odd choice for your charity, with so many others in real need. Beth's not here, then?

SIMON. No, she's taken some of her foreign students to Canterbury.

STEPHEN. Did she go with that teacher she was telling Teresa about?

SIMON. Chap called Ned?

STEPHEN. Yes.

SIMON. Yes.

STEPHEN. What do you think of him?

SIMON. Oh, rather a wry, sad little fellow. Bit of a failure, I'd say, from what I've seen of him.

STEPHEN. A failure? In what way?

SIMON. Oh, you know, teaching English to foreigners.

STEPHEN. So does Beth.

SIMON. True, but Beth isn't a middle-aged man with ginger hair, a pigeon-toed gait, a depressed-looking wife and four children to boot.

STEPHEN. You know, sometimes I can't help wondering how people describe me. A middle-aged public school teacher with five children to boot. A bit of a failure too, eh? Anyhow, that's how I feel today.

SIMON. Why, what's the matter?

STEPHEN. That damned interview.

SIMON. Interview?

STEPHEN. For the Assistant Headmastership. You'd forgotten then!

SIMON. No, no of *course* I hadn't. When is it exactly?

STEPHEN (*looks at him*). Yesterday.

SIMON. Good God! Was it really? Well, what happened?

STEPHEN. I didn't get it.

SIMON. Well, who did?

STEPHEN. A chap called MacGregor. And quite right too, as he's already Assistant Headmaster of a small public school in Edinburgh, very capable, written a couple of text books - in other words he's simply the better man for the job.

SIMON. I don't see what that's got to do with it. I don't know how your Headmaster had the face to tell you.

STEPHEN. Oh, he didn't. Nobody's had the face or the grace. Yet.

SIMON. Then how do you know he's got it.

STEPHEN. It was written all over MacGregor. I've never seen anyone so perky after an interview.

SIMON. Oh good God, is that all? Of course he was perky. He's a Scot isn't he? They're always perky. Except when they're doleful. Usually they're both at once.

STEPHEN. If you'd seen him come bouncing down the library steps.

SIMON. In my experience a bouncing candidate is a rejected candidate. No, no, Steve, my money's on your paddle feet. (*He sits.*)

STEPHEN. Even though my interview lasted a mere half hour

although his lasted fifty-seven minutes? Even though I fluffed my mere half hour, and before a hostile board. Do you know, one of the Governors couldn't get over the fact that I'd taken my degree at Reading. He was unable to grasp that Reading was a university even, he referred to it as if it were some cut-price institution where I'd scraped up some - some diploma on the cheap. MacGregor went to Oxford, needless to say.

SIMON. Did he? Which college?

STEPHEN. And then another Governor harped on the number of our children - he kept saying *five* children, eh? Like that. Five children, eh? As if I'd had - I don't know - five - five -

SIMON. Cheques returned.

STEPHEN. What?

SIMON. That's what you made it sound as if he sounded as if he were saying.

STEPHEN. Anyway, there were the two Governors manifestly hostile.

SIMON. Out of how many?

STEPHEN. Two.

SIMON. Ah, but then your Headmaster was on your side.

STEPHEN. Perhaps. (*Pause.*) At least until I succeeded in putting him off.

SIMON. How?

STEPHEN. By doing something I haven't done since I was twelve years old.

SIMON (*after a pause*). Can you be more specific?

STEPHEN. You will of course laugh, for which I shan't of course blame you, but I'm not sure that I can stand it if you do laugh at the moment. It was something very trivial, but also very embarrassing. (*Pause.*) You see, the Governor who didn't feel Reading was up to snuff had a rather low, husky voice, and towards the end I bent forward, rather sharply, to catch something he said, and this movement caused me to fart.

They stare levelly at each other. SIMON'S *face is completely composed.*

SIMON. You haven't farted since you were twelve?

STEPHEN. In public, I meant.

SIMON. Oh. Loudly?

STEPHEN. It sounded to me like a pistol shot.

SIMON. The question, of course, is what it sounded like to Headmaster.

STEPHEN. Like a fart, I should think.

SIMON. Oh, he probably found it sympathetically human, you've no grounds for believing he'd hold anything so accidental against you, surely?

STEPHEN. I don't know, I simply don't know. (*He gets up.*) But afterwards when he had us around for some of his wife's herbal coffee -

SIMON. Herbal coffee?

STEPHEN. They paid far more attention to MacGregor than they did to me. I had to struggle to keep my end up. Headmaster was distinctly aloof in his manner - and MacGregor, of course, was relaxed and I suppose a fair man would call it charming.

SIMON. What herbs does she use?

STEPHEN. What? What's that got to do with it? How would I know.

SIMON. Sorry, I was just trying to imagine the - the setting, so to speak.

STEPHEN. You know, what really hurts is that I can't complain that it's unfair. MacGregor really is better qualified, quite obviously an admirable bloke. But what I do resent, and can't help resenting, is the edge Oxford gives him - the simple fact that he went there improves his chances - but I suppose that's the way of the world, isn't it? Almost everybody goes along with it, don't they?

SIMON. Oh, I don't know -

STEPHEN. Of course you know. You subscribe to it yourself, don't you?

SIMON. Certainly not. Why should I?

STEPHEN. Because you went to Oxford yourself.

SIMON. Good God, so what?

STEPHEN. Well, how many other members of your editorial board also went there.

SIMON. Only five.

STEPHEN. Out of how many?

SIMON. Eight.

STEPHEN. And where did the other three go, Cambridge?

SIMON. Only two of them.

STEPHEN. And so only *one* of the nine went elsewhere?

SIMON. No, he didn't go anywhere. He's the Chairman's son.

STEPHEN. I think that proves my point.

SIMON. It proves merely that our editorial board is composed of Oxford and Cambridge graduates, and a half-wit. It proves absolutely nothing about your chances of beating MacDonald to the Assistant Headmastership. And it's my view that poor old MacDonald, whether he be Oxford MacDonald or Cambridge MacDonald or Reading MacDonald or plain Edinburgh MacDonald -

STEPHEN. MacGregor.

SIMON. What?

STEPHEN. His name happens to be MacGregor.

SIMON. Absolutely. Has no chance at all. Even if they do believe you have too few qualifications and too many children, even if they suspect that your single fart heralds chronic incontinence, they'll still have to appoint you. And if they've been extra courteous to MacDonald it's only to compensate him for coming all the way from Edinburgh for a London rebuff. (*Stands up.*)

STEPHEN. Actually it would be better, if you don't mind, not to try and jolly me along with reasons and reassurances. I shall have to face the disappointment sooner or later, and I'd rather do it sooner - wouldn't you?

SIMON. No, I have a distinct preference for later, myself. I really do think you'll get it you know.

STEPHEN. Yes, well thanks anyway. I'd better get back. What time's your friend coming?

SIMON. What friend?

STEPHEN. When I phoned and asked whether I could come round, you said it mightn't be worth my while as you were expecting a friend.

SIMON. Good God! Yes. Still, he's one of those people who never turns up when expected. So if I remember to expect him I should be all right.

STEPHEN. You mean you don't want him to turn up? Who is he anyway?

SIMON. Jeff Golding.

STEPHEN. Oh *him*! Yes, well I must say that piece he wrote in one of last week's Sundays, on censorship and children - I've never read anything so posturingly half-baked.

SIMON. Oh, I doubt if he was posturing, he really is half-baked.

STEPHEN. I shall never forget - never - how he ruined the dinner party - the one time I met him - his drunkenness and his appalling behaviour. And I shall particularly never forget his announcing that people - he meant me, of course - only went into public school teaching because they were latent pederasts.

SIMON. Good God, what did you say?

STEPHEN. I told him to take it back.

SIMON. And did he?

STEPHEN. He offered to take back the latent, and congratulated me on my luck. That was his idea of badinage. By God I don't often lose control but I made a point of cornering him in the hall when he was leaving. I got him by the lapels and warned him that I'd a good mind to beat some manners into him. If Teresa hadn't happened to come out of the lavatory just then - she'd rushed in there in tears - I might have done him some damage. I've never told you that bit before, have I?

SIMON. You haven't told me any of it before, it's very amusing. Tell me, who gave this memorable dinner party?

STEPHEN. You did.

SIMON. Did I really? I don't remember it. It must have been a long time ago.

STEPHEN. Yes, but I have a feeling your friend Jeff Golding will remember it all right.

The front door slams and JEFF GOLDING *enters left.*

JEFF. Simon - ah, there you are.

There is a pause.

Weren't you expecting me?

SIMON. I most certainly was. Oh, my brother Stephen - Jeff Golding. I believe you know each other.

STEPHEN. We do indeed.

JEFF. Really? Sorry, 'fraid I don't remember.

STEPHEN. A dinner party Simon gave - some years ago.

JEFF (*clearly not remembering at all*). Nice to see you again. Could I have a scotch please? (*To* SIMON.)

SIMON. Of course. (*Goes to the drinks table.*) Steve?

STEPHEN. No thank you.

JEFF (*collapses into a chair*). Christ! Christ! I've just had a session at the Beeb, taping a piece with Bugger Lampwith. I've got the goods on him at last.

STEPHEN. Lampwith. Isn't he a poet?

JEFF. Not even. He's an Australian. A closet Australian. Went to Oxford instead of Earl's Court. Thinks it makes him one of us. Still, I got him out of his closet with his vowels around his tonsils, once or twice. Thrice, actually. (*Laughs at the recollection.*)

STEPHEN. What exactly have you got against him?

JEFF. Isn't that enough?

STEPHEN. Simply that he's an Australian?

JEFF. They're all right as dentists.

STEPHEN. But could you please explain to me why you have it in for Australians.

JEFF. Once you let them into literature they lower the property values.

STEPHEN. Really? How?

JEFF. They're too fertile, scribble, scribble, scribble like little Gibbons. They breed whole articles out of small reviews, don't mind what work they do, go from sports journalists to movie critics to novelists to poets to television pundits, and furthermore they don't mind how little they get paid as long as they fill our space. So you see if there weren't any Australians around sods like me wouldn't end up having to flog our crap to the Radio Times and even the Shiterary Supplement, let alone spend Saturday morning interviewing buggers like Bugger Lampwith.

STEPHEN. We've got half a dozen Australian boys in our school at the moment. They're not only friendly, frank and outgoing, they're also intelligent and very hard-working.

JEFF. Exactly, the little buggers. Hey! (*To* SIMON.) Roger's been going around telling people I can't face him since my review of his turgid little turd of a novel. Have you read it?

SIMON. Which?

JEFF. My review - first things first.

SIMON. Yes, I did.

JEFF. Well?

SIMON. Some good jokes, I thought.

JEFF. Weren't there? And what did you honestly, frankly and actually think of his turd?

SIMON. I haven't read it.

JEFF. Didn't you publish it?

SIMON. Yes.

JEFF. Well, if you ask me, the blokie you got to write the blurb hadn't read it either, bloody sloppy piece of crap, who did it anyway?

SIMON. Actually I did.

JEFF. D'you know what it bloody is - I'll tell you what it bloody is - I wish I'd come out with it straight when I wrote about it - it's a piece of - *literature*, that's what it bloody is!

STEPHEN. You don't like literature?

JEFF (*a pause*). I don't like literature, no.

STEPHEN. Why not?

JEFF. Because it's a bloody boring racket.

STEPHEN. You think literature is a *racket*?

JEFF. Are you in it too?

STEPHEN. I happen to teach it, it so happens.

JEFF. Does it, Christ! To whom?

STEPHEN. Sixth formers. At Amplesides.

JEFF. What's Amplesides?

STEPHEN. It happens to be a public school.

JEFF. Does it? Major or minor?

STEPHEN. Let's just say that it's a good one, if you don't mind.

JEFF. I don't mind saying it even if it's not. It's a good one. Christ, I can't remember when I last met a public school teacher.

STEPHEN. Probably when you last met me.

JEFF. But I don't remember that, don't forget.

STEPHEN. Would you like me to remind you? I'm the latent pederast.

JEFF (*after a pause*). Then you're in the right job.

STEPHEN (*to* SIMON). I think I'd better go. Before I do something I regret. (*Turns and goes out through kitchen.*)

SIMON. Oh right. (*Making an attempt to follow* STEPHEN.) Love to Teresa and the kids. (*Calling it out.*)

Sound of door slamming. JEFF *helps himself to another scotch.*

JEFF. Seems a real sweetie, what's he like in real life?

SIMON. Not as stupid as he seems.

JEFF. That still leaves him a lot of room to be stupid in.

SIMON. He *is* my brother.

JEFF. I'm very sorry.

SIMON. Actually, the last time he met you, he offered to fight you.

JEFF. Then he's matured since then. Where's Beth?

SIMON. Gone to Canterbury.

JEFF. With her woggies?

SIMON. Yes.

JEFF. Never seem to see her these days. You two still all right, I take it?

SIMON. Yes, thanks.

JEFF. Christ, you're lucky, don't know how you do it. She's so bloody attractive of course, as well as nice and intelligent. I suppose that helps.

SIMON. Yes, it does really.

JEFF. And she's got that funny little moral streak in her - she doesn't altogether approve of me, I get the feeling. Even after all these years. Christ, women! Listen there's something I want to talk to you about, and I'll just lay down the guide-lines of your response. What I want from you is an attentive face and a cocked ear, the good old-fashioned friendly sympathy and concern for which you're celebrated, O bloody K?

SIMON. Well, I'll do my best.

JEFF. Remember Gwendoline?

SIMON. Gwendoline, no. Have I met her?

JEFF. Hundreds of times.

SIMON. Really, where?

JEFF. With me.

SIMON. Oh. Which one was she - to tell you the truth, Jeff, there've been so many that the only one I still have the slightest recollection of is your ex-wife.

JEFF. Are you sure?

SIMON. Absolutely.

JEFF. Well, that was Gwendoline.

SIMON. Oh, I thought her name was Gwynyth.

JEFF. Why?

SIMON. What?

JEFF. Why should you think her name was Gwynyth?

SIMON. Wasn't she Welsh?

JEFF. No, she bloody was not Welsh.

SIMON. Well, I haven't seen her for years, don't forget, not since

the afternoon you threw your drink in her face and walked out
on her.

JEFF. And that's all you remember?

SIMON. Well, it *did* happen in my flat, a lunch party you asked
me to give so that you could meet the then Arts Editor of the
Sunday Times, and you did leave her sobbing on my bed,
into my pillow, with the stink of scotch everywhere -

JEFF. Don't you remember anything else about my Gwendoline
days, for Christ's sake? What I used to tell you about her?

SIMON (*thinks*). Yes. You used to tell me that she was the
stupidest woman I'd ever met.

JEFF. *You'd* ever met.

SIMON. Yes.

JEFF. And was she?

SIMON. Yes.

JEFF. Well, you've met some stupider since, haven't you?

SIMON. Probably, but fortunately I can't remember them either.

JEFF. So you rather despised my poor old Gwendoline, did you?

SIMON. Absolutely. So did you.

JEFF. Then why do you think I married her?

SIMON. Because of the sex.

JEFF. Did I tell you that too?

SIMON. No, you told her that, once or twice, in front of me.

JEFF. Christ, what a bloody swine of a fool I was. (*Pours himself
another drink.*) Well, now I'm suffering for it, aren't I? Listen,
a few months ago I bumped into her in Oxford Street. I
hadn't given her a thought in all that time, and suddenly
there we were, face to face, looking at each other. For a full
minute just looking. And do you know something, she cried.
And I felt as if we were - Christ, you know - still married.
But in the very first days of it, when we couldn't keep our
hands off each other. In a matter of minutes.

SIMON. Minutes?

JEFF. Minutes. Bloody minutes. All over each other.

SIMON. In *Oxford* Street.

JEFF. I'll tell you - I put my hand out, very slowly, and stroked her cheek. The tears were running down, her mouth was trembling - and she took my hand and pressed it against her cheek. Then I took her to Nick's flat - he's still in hospital by the way.

SIMON. Really? I didn't know he'd gone in.

JEFF. They're trying aversion therapy this time, but it won't do any good. He's so bloody addictive that he'll come out hooked on the cure and still stay hooked on the gin, poor sod. Saline chasers. Anyway, I took her to Nick's, and had her, and had her, and had her. Christ! And when she left what do you think I did?

SIMON. Slept, I should think.

JEFF. I cried, that's what I did. Didn't want her to leave me, you see. I'm in love with her. I think I love her. And since then there have been times when I've thought I even liked her. Well?

SIMON. Well Jeff, that's marvellous. Really marvellous.

JEFF. Oh yes, bloody marvellous to discover that you want to marry your ex-wife.

SIMON. But why ever not? It just confirms that you were right the first time. Why not marry her?

JEFF (*taking another drink*). Because she's got a new bloody husband, that's why. In fact not so new, five years old. A bloody don in Cambridge called Manfred. Christ knows why he had to go and *marry* her!

SIMON. Perhaps he likes sex too.

JEFF. According to Gwen he likes TV situation comedies, football matches, wrestling, comic books, horror films and sadistic thrillers, but not sex.

SIMON. What does he teach?

JEFF. Moral sciences.

SIMON. Then there's your answer. Philosophers have a long tradition of marrying stupid women, from Socrates on. They think it clever. Does she love him?

JEFF. Of course she does, she loves everyone. But she loves me most. Except for their bloody child. She bloody dotes on the bloody child.

SIMON. Oh. How old is it?

JEFF. Two - three - four - that sort of age.

SIMON. Boy or girl?

JEFF. Can't really tell. The one time I saw it, through my car window, it was trotting into its nursery school with its arm over its face, like a mobster going to the grand jury.

SIMON. Haven't you asked Gwen which it is?

JEFF. Yes, but only to show interest. Anyway, what does it matter, what matters is she won't leave Manfred because of it. She's *my* wife, not his, I had her first, and she admits as much, she'll always be mine, but all I get of her is two goes a week when I drive up to Cambridge - Tuesdays and Thursdays in the afternoon when Manfred's conducting seminars. In the rooms of some smartie-boots theologian.

SIMON (*pacing up and down*). Do you mean Manfred conducts his seminars in the rooms of some smartie-boots theologian or you have Gwen in the rooms of some smartie-boots theologian?

JEFF. I have Gwen there. He's a friend of Manfred's you see.

SIMON. So Manfred's asked him to let you use his rooms?

JEFF. Oh no, Manfred doesn't know anything about it. Or about me. No, smartie-boots seems to have some idea that it's part of his job to encourage what he calls sin. Oh Christ, you know the type, a squalid little Anglican queen of a pimp the little sod. Turns my stomach. (*Adds more scotch.*) Christ, you know, Simon, you want to know something about me?

SIMON. What? (*Sinks into an armchair.*)

JEFF. I'm English, yes, English to my marrow's marrow. After years of buggering about as a cosmopolitan literateur, going to PEN conferences in Warsaw, hob-nobbing with Frog poets and Eyetye essaysists, German novelists and Greek composers, I suddenly realise I hate the lot of them. Furthermore I detest women, love men, loathe queers. D'you know when I'm really at bloody peace with myself? When I'm caught in a traffic jam on an English road, under an English heaven - somewhere between London and Cambridge, on my way to Gwen, on my way back from her, rain sliding down the window, engine humming, dreaming - dreaming of what's past or is to come.

Wrapped in the anticipation of the memory, no, the anticipation of the memory. (*Pause.*) Oh Christ - it's my actual bloody opinion that this sad little, bloody little country of ours is finished at last. Bloody finished at last. Yes, it truly is bloody well actually finished at last. I mean that. Had the VAT man around the other day. That's what we get now instead of the muffin man. I remember the muffin men, I'm old enough to remember the muffin men. Their bells and smells and lighting of the lamps - do you remember? Sometimes I even remember hansom cabs and crinoline, the music halls and Hobbes and Sutcliffe . . . (*Smiles.*) Or the memory of the anticipation, I suppose. Stu Lampwith. Christ, the bugger! (*Pause.*) Well Christ - I suppose I'd better go and write my piece. (*He gets to his feet.*) Did I tell you what that cold-hearted bitch said last night, in bed? Christ!

SIMON. Who?

JEFF. What?

SIMON. What cold-hearted bitch?

JEFF. Davina. (*Takes another scotch.*)

SIMON. Davina?

JEFF. You don't know about Davina?

SIMON (*wearily*). No.

JEFF. You haven't met her?

SIMON. No, no - I don't think -

JEFF. But Christ, I've got to tell you about bitch Davina. (*Sits down.*)

SIMON. Why?

JEFF. Because she is actually and completely the most utterly and totally - (*Lifts his hand.*)

There is a ring at the door-bell.

What?

SIMON. Just a minute, Jeff. (*Goes to the door, opens it.*)

DAVINA. Hello, is Jeff here, by any chance? (JEFF *groans in recognition and sits down on the sofa.*)

SIMON. Yes, yes he is. Come in.

(DAVINA *enters.* JEFF *ignores her.*)

DAVINA. I'm Davina Saunders. (*To* SIMON.)

SIMON. I'm Simon Hench.

DAVINA. I know.

There is a pause.

SIMON. Would you like a drink?

DAVINA. Small gin and bitters, please.

SIMON *goes across to the drinks table.*

JEFF. How did you know I was here?

DAVINA. You said you would be.

JEFF. Why did I tell you?

DAVINA. Because I asked you.

JEFF. But why did I tell you. Because you see, I wanted a quiet conversation with my friend, Simon, you see.

DAVINA. You're all right then, are you?

JEFF. What? (*A pause.* SIMON *brings* DAVINA *her drink.*)

DAVINA. How did the interview go?

JEFF. All right.

DAVINA. What's he like?

JEFF. Who?

DAVINA. Bugger Lampwith.

JEFF. OK.

DAVINA. What's OK about him?

JEFF. He's all right.

DAVINA. Good.

JEFF. What do you mean, good?

DAVINA. That he's all right. (*Sits down.*)

JEFF. Well, what d'you want me to say, you follow me across bloody London, you turn up when I'm having a private bloody conversation with my old friend Simon, you're scarcely in the room before you ask me whether I'm drunk -

DAVINA. As a matter of sober precision, I did not ask you

whether you were drunk. I asked you whether you were all right.

JEFF. Then as a matter of drunken precision, no, I'm not all right, I'm drunk.

DAVINA. That's surprising, as with you being all right and being drunk are usually precisely synonymous.

JEFF. But now you're here, aren't you, and that alters everything, doesn't it?

DAVINA. Does it?

JEFF. I thought you were going to spend the morning at the British Bloody Museum. I thought we'd agreed not to see each other for a day or two, or even a year or two -

There is a pause.

SIMON. What are you doing at the BM, some research?

JEFF. That's what she's doing. On Major Bloody Barttelot. Got the idea from *my* review of that Life of Stanley - naturally.

SIMON. Really, and who is Major Bloody Barttelot?

DAVINA. Major Barttelot went with Stanley to the Congo, was left in a camp to guard the Rear Column, and ended up flogging, shooting, and even, so the story goes, eating the natives.

JEFF. Pleasant work for a woman, eh?

SIMON. Major Barttelot was a *woman*?

DAVINA. He was an English gentleman. Although he did find it pleasant work from what I've discovered, yes.

SIMON. Really? And are you planning a book?

JEFF. Of course she is, cannibalism, sadism, doing down England all at the same time, how can it miss? Why do you think she's on to it?

SIMON. I must say it sounds quite fascinating. Who's your publisher?

DAVINA. I haven't got one yet.

JEFF. Is that what summoned you away from the BM, the chance of drawing up a contract with my old friend, the publisher Simon? (*Refills his glass.*)

DAVINA. Actually, I haven't been to the BM this morning. I've been on the telephone. And what summoned me here was first that I wanted to give you your key back. (*Throws it over to him.*)

JEFF (*makes no attempt to catch it*). Thank you.

DAVINA. And secondly to tell you about the telephone call.

JEFF. What? Who was it?

DAVINA. Your ex-wife's husband. Manfred.

JEFF. What did he want?

DAVINA. You.

JEFF. Why?

DAVINA. He wanted you to know the contents of Gwendoline's suicide letter.

JEFF (*after a pause*). What? Gwendoline - what - Gwen's dead!

SIMON. Good God!

DAVINA. No.

JEFF. But she tried - tried to commit suicide?

DAVINA. Apparently.

JEFF. What do you mean apparently, you mean she failed?

DAVINA. Oh, I'd say she succeeded. At least to the extent that Manfred was hysterical, I had a wastefully boring morning on the telephone, and you look almost sober. What more could she expect from a mere bid, after all?

JEFF. For Christ sake, what happened, what actually happened?

DAVINA. Well, Manfred's narrative was a trifle rhapsodic.

JEFF. But you said there was a letter.

DAVINA. He only read out the opening sentences - he was too embarrassed by them to go on.

JEFF. Embarrassed by what?

DAVINA. Oh, Gwendoline's epistolary style, I should think. It was rather shaming.

JEFF. Look, where is she?

DAVINA. In that hospital in Cambridge probably. And if you're thinking of going up there, you should reflect that Manfred is looking forward to beating you to a pulp. A *bloody* pulp was his phrase, and unlike yourself he seems to use the word literally, rather than for rhetorical effect or as drunken punctuation. I like people who express themselves limpidly (*To* SIMON.) under stress, don't you?

JEFF (*throws his drink at her, splashing her blouse, etc.*). Is that limpid enough for you?

DAVINA. No, tritely theatrical, as usual. But if you're absolutely determined to go, and you might as well because what else have you to do? I advise you not to drive. Otherwise you may have to make do with one of the hospitals *en route*.

SIMON. Yes, you really shouldn't drive, Jeff . . .

JEFF *turns, goes out, left, slamming the door. There is a pause.*

I'll get you something to wipe your shirt –

DAVINA. Don't bother, it's far too wet. But another drink please. (*Hands him her glass.*)

SIMON. Of course.

Takes it, goes to the drinks table.
DAVINA *takes off her shirt and throws it over a chair. She is bra-less. She goes to the large wall mirror, and dries herself with a handkerchief from her bag.*
SIMON *turns with the drink, looks at* DAVINA, *falters slightly, then brings her her drink.*

DAVINA. God, what a stupid man, don't you think?

SIMON. Well, a bit excitable at times, perhaps.

DAVINA. No, stupid really, and in an all-round way. You know, when I was at Oxford one used to take his articles quite seriously – not very seriously but quite. But now of course one sees that his facility, though it may pass in the Arts pages as intelligence and originality, was something merely cultivated in late adolescence for the examination halls. He hasn't developed, in fact his Gwendoline syndrome makes it evident that he's regressed. Furthermore his drunken bravado quickly ceases to be amusing, on top of which he's a fourth-rate fuck.

SIMON. Oh well, perhaps he's kind to animals.

DAVINA (*sitting on the sofa*). To think I thought he might be of some use to me. But of course he's out of the habit, if he was ever in it, of talking to women who like to think and therefore talk concisely, for whom intelligence does actually involve judgement, and for whom judgement concludes in discrimination. Hence the appeal, I suppose, of a pair of tits from which he can dangle, with closed eyes and infantile gurglings. Especially if he has to get to them furtively, with a sense of not being allowed. Yes, stupid, don't you agree?

SIMON. Did you really go to Oxford?

DAVINA. Came down two years ago, why?

SIMON. From your style you sound more as if you went to Cambridge.

DAVINA. Anyway, he's nicely gone, you will admit, and four bad weeks have been satisfactorily concluded.

SIMON. Aren't you a little worried about him, though?

DAVINA. Why should I be?

SIMON. Well, Manfred did threaten to beat him to a bloody pulp, after all. And it may not be an idle boast. Men whose wives attempt suicide because of other men sometimes become quite animated, even if they are moral scientists.

DAVINA. Oh, I think the wretched Manfred will be more bewildered than belligerent. I composed that fiction between Great Russell Street and here. Of course I didn't know until I met his glassy gaze and received his boorish welcome whether I was actually going to work it through. It was quite thrilling, don't you think?

SIMON. You mean, Gwendoline didn't try to commit suicide?

DAVINA. Surely you don't imagine that *that* complacent old cow would attempt even an attempted suicide?

SIMON. Why did you do it?

DAVINA. Spite of course. Well, he told me he wanted to bring it all to a climax, although he wanted no such thing of course, prolonged and squalid messes that lead least of all to climaxes being his method, so my revenge has been to provide him with one that should be exactly in character - prolonged, squalid and utterly messy even by Cambridge standards, don't you think? *You're* married, aren't you? To Beth, isn't it?

SIMON. That's right.

DAVINA. I've only just realized she isn't here is she?

SIMON. Well, I suppose that's better than just realizing she was, isn't it?

DAVINA. I'd like to have met her. I've heard a great deal about you both, you mainly, of course. Are you two as imperturbably, not to say implacably *married* and he and everyone else says?

SIMON. I hope so.

DAVINA. And that you've never been unfaithful to Beth, at at least as far as Jeff knows.

SIMON. Certainly never that far.

DAVINA. Don't you even fancy other women?

SIMON (*sits in the armchair*). My not sleeping with other women has absolutely nothing to do with not fancying them. Although I do make a particular point of not sleeping with women I don't fancy.

DAVINA. That's meant for me, is it?

SIMON. Good God, not at all.

DAVINA. You mean you do fancy me?

SIMON. I didn't mean that either.

DAVINA. But do you fancy me?

SIMON. Yes.

DAVINA. But you don't like me?

SIMON. No.

DAVINA. Ah, then do you fancy me *because* you *don't* like me? Some complicated set of manly mechanisms of that sort, is it?

SIMON. No, very simple ones that Jeff, for instance, would fully appreciate. I fancy you because of your breasts, you see. I'm revolted by your conversation and appalled by your behaviour. I think you're possibly the most egocentrically unpleasant woman I've ever met, but I have a yearning for your breasts. I'd like to dangle from them too, with my eyes closed and doubtless emitting infantile gurglings. Furthermore they look deceptively hospitable.

DAVINA. If they look deceptively hospitable, they're deceiving you. (*Comes over and sits on the arm of his chair.*) You're very welcome to a nuzzle (*Pause.*) Go on then. And then we'll see what *you* can do.

> SIMON *sits, hesitating for a moment, then gets up, gets* DAVINA'S *shirt, hands it to her.*

Because of Beth?

SIMON. This is her house, as much as mine. It's *our* house, don't you see?

DAVINA. Fidelity means so much to you?

SIMON. Let's say rather more to me than a suck and a fuck with the likes of you. So, comes to that, does Jeff.

DAVINA. Yes, well I suppose that's to be expected in a friend of his. He doesn't begin to exist and nor do you.

SIMON. That's excellent. Because I haven't the slightest intention of letting you invent me.

DAVINA. And what about my Barttelot book?

SIMON. There I'm sure we shall understand each other. If it's any good, I shall be delighted to publish it. And if you've any sense, and you've got a hideous sight too much, you'll be delighted to let me. I shall give you the best advance available in London, arrange an excellent deal with an American publisher, and I shall see that it's edited to your advantage as well as ours. If it's any good.

DAVINA. That means more to me than being sucked at and fucked by the likes of you.

> *They smile.* DAVINA *turns and goes out.*
> SIMON, *with the air of a man celebrating, picks up the keys and glasses, puts them away. Makes to go to the gramophone, stops, goes to the telephone answering machine.*

SIMON (*records*). 348-0720, Simon Hench on an answering machine. I shall be otherwise engaged for the rest of the day. If you have a message for either myself or for Beth could you please wait until after the high-pitched tone, and if that hasn't put you off, speak. Thank you.

> *Puts the button down, then goes over to the gramophone, bends over to put a record on.*

DAVE *enters*, SIMON *freezes, turns.*

DAVE. She didn't show.

SIMON. What?

DAVE. Suzy. My girl. She didn't show. You know what I'd like to do now, I'd like to get really pissed, that's what I'd like to do.

SIMON. I don't blame you, and furthermore, why don't you? You'll still catch the pubs if you hurry -

DAVE. Well, I'm a bit short, you see.

SIMON. But didn't you have a few pounds -

DAVE. Yeah, well I spent those.

SIMON. Oh, what on?

DAVE. Usual sort of stuff.

SIMON. Well then, let me. (*Pause.*) I've got just the thing.

Goes to the drinks table fishes behind, takes out a bottle of Cyprus sherry.

Here. Go on, one of Beth's students gave it to her - it's yours. (*Hands it to* DAVE.) A Cyprus sherry. Nice and sweet. Now you settle down in some dark corner, with a receptacle by your side, and forget yourself completely. That's what I'd want to do if I were you. (*Points him towards the door.*)

DAVE *goes out.* SIMON *turns back to the hi-fi. Voices in the hall.*

DAVE (*opens the door*). Bloke here for you. (*Withdraws.*)

SIMON. What? (*Turns.*)

WOOD (*enters*). Mr Hench?

SIMON. Yes.

WOOD. Can you spare me a few minutes? My name is Wood. Bernard Wood.

SIMON (*as if recognising the name, then checks it*). Oh?

WOOD. It means something to you, then?

SIMON. No, just an echo. Of Birnam Wood, it must be, coming to Dunsinane. No, I'm very sorry, it doesn't. Should it?

WOOD. You don't recognise me either, I take it?

SIMON. No, I'm afraid not. Should I?

WOOD. We went to school together.

SIMON. Did we really, Wundale?

WOOD. Yes. Wundale. I was all of three years ahead of you, but I recall you. It should be the other way around, shouldn't it? But then *you* were very distinctive.

SIMON. Was I really, in what way?

WOOD (*after a little pause*). Oh, as the sexy little boy that all the glamorous boys of my year slept with.

SIMON (*after a pause*). But you didn't?

WOOD. No.

SIMON. Well, I do hope you haven't come to make good, because it's too late, I'm afraid. The phase is over, by some decades. (*Little pause, then with an effort at courtesy.*) I'm sure I would have remembered you, though, if we had slept together.

WOOD. Well, perhaps your brother - Stephen, isn't it - would remember me as we were in the same year, how is he?

SIMON. Oh, very well.

WOOD. Married, with children?

SIMON. Yes.

WOOD. And you're married?

SIMON. Yes.

WOOD. Good. Children?

SIMON. No.

WOOD. Why not?

SIMON. There isn't enough room. What about you?

WOOD. Oh, as you might expect of someone like me. Married with children.

There is a pause.

SIMON. Well . . . um - you said there was something - ?

WOOD. Yes, there is. It's of a rather personal - embarrassing nature.

Pause.

SIMON (*unenthusiastically*). Would a drink help?

WOOD. Oh, that's very kind. Some sherry would be nice, if you have it.

SIMON. Yes, I have it.

WOOD. Then some sherry if I may.

SIMON. Yes, you may. (*Pours* WOOD *a sherry.*)

WOOD. My many thanks. Your very good health. I thought you might have heard my name the day before yesterday.

SIMON. Oh, in what context?

WOOD. From my girl, Joanna. In your office, at about six in the evening.

SIMON. Joanna?

WOOD. She came to see you about getting work in publishing. She's only just left art school, but you were kind enough to give her an appointment.

SIMON. Oh yes, yes. I do remember a girl - I'm terrible about names, a nice girl, I thought.

WOOD. Thank you. How did your meeting go? Just between us?

SIMON. Well, I thought she was really quite promising.

WOOD. But you didn't make her any promises.

SIMON. Well, no, I'm afraid I couldn't. What work of hers she showed me struck me as a - a trifle over-expressive for our needs. (*Pause.*) Why, is her version of our, um, talk different, in any way?

WOOD. She hasn't said anything about it at all.

SIMON. I see. And you've come to me to find out about her potential?

WOOD. Not really, no. I've come to ask you if you know where she is.

SIMON. Have you lost her then?

WOOD. She hasn't been home since I dropped her off at your office.

SIMON. Well, I'm very sorry, but I haven't seen her since she left my office.

WOOD. I only have one rule with her, that she come home at night. Failing that, that at least she let me know where or with whom she is spending the night. Failing that, that at least she telephone me first thing in the morning. Could I be more unreasonably reasonable? So before doing the rounds among her pals, from Ladbroke Grove to Earls Court, I thought it might be worth finding out from you if she let anything slip about her plans.

SIMON. Nothing that I can remember.

WOOD. She didn't mention any particular friend or boy-friend?

SIMON. Just the usual references to this drip and that drip in the modern manner. Look, from what one makes out of today's youth, isn't it likely that she'll come home when she feels in the mood or wants a good meal, eh?

WOOD. I suppose so.

SIMON. I can quite understand your worry -

WOOD. Can you? No, I don't think you can.

SIMON. No, perhaps not. But I really don't see how I can help you any further.

WOOD. Did you have it off with her?

SIMON. What? *What*?

WOOD. Did you have it off with her?

SIMON. Look, Wood, whatever your anxiety about your daughter, I really don't think, old chap, that you should insinuate yourself into people's homes and put a question like that to them. I mean, good God, you can't possibly expect me to dignify it with an answer, can you?

WOOD. In other words, you did.

SIMON (*after a long pause*). In other words, I'm afraid I did. Yes. Sorry, old chap.

Curtain.

Act Two

Curtain up on exactly same scene, **WOOD** *and* SIMON *in exactly the same postures. There is a pause.*

WOOD. Tell me, does your wife know you do this sort of thing?

SIMON. Why, are you going to tell her?

WOOD. Oh, I'm not a sneak. Besides, Joanna would never forgive me. She'd have told me herself, you know, She always does. She thinks it's good for me to know what she and her pals get up to. Do you do it often. (*Smiling.*)

SIMON. Reasonably often. Or unreasonably, depending on one's point of view.

WOOD. And always with girls of my Joanna's age?

SIMON. There or thereabouts, yes.

WOOD. Because you don't love your wife?

SIMON. No, because I do. I make a point, you see, of not sleeping with friends, or the wives of friends, or acquaintances even. No one in our circle. Relationships there can be awkward enough -

WOOD. It's a sort of code, is it?

SIMON. No doubt it seems a rather squalid one, to you.

WOOD. So that's why you chose my Joanna, is it?

SIMON. I didn't really choose her, you know. She came into my office, and we looked at her work, and talked -

WOOD. Until everybody else had gone. You decided, in other words, that she was an easy lay. And wouldn't make any fuss, afterwards.

SIMON. I also realized that I couldn't possibly do her any harm.

WOOD. What about the clap? (*Pause.*) I think I have a right to know.

SIMON. I keep some pills at my office.

WOOD. So your post-coital period together was passed gobbling down anti VD pills.

SIMON. One doesn't exactly gobble them - one swallows them, as one might digestive tablets.

WOOD. What about going back to your wife, reeking of sex?

SIMON. What?

WOOD. What do you do about the stench of your adulteries?

SIMON. I confess I find this enquiry into method rather depressing. I'd willingly settle for a burst of parental outrage -

WOOD. And I'd far rather satisfy my curiosity. Won't you please tell me?

SIMON. Very well. I stop off at my squash club, play a few points with the professional, then have a shower.

WOOD. But you don't suffer from any guilt afterwards? No post-coital distress, no angst or even embarrassment?

SIMON. Not unless this counts as afterwards.

WOOD. So really, only your sexual tastes have changed, your moral organism has survived intact ince the days when you were that lucky sod, the Wundale Tart?

SIMON. Look, are you here because I slept around at thirteen, with the attractive boys of your year, or because I sleep around with attractive girls of your daughter's generation, at thirty-nine. Good God Wood, I'm beginning to find something frankly Mediterranean in this obsession with your child's sex-life - and mine - after all, let's face it, in the grand scheme of things, nothing much has happened, and in the Anglo-Saxon scheme of things, your daughter's well over the age of consent. That may sound brutal, but it's also true.

WOOD. Except in one important point. She's not my daughter.

SIMON. What? What is she then?

WOOD. My (*Hesitates.*) fiancée.

SIMON. Is it worth my saying sorry over again, or will my earlier apologies serve. (*Pause.*) But I thought you said her name was Wood -

WOOD. Yes.

SIMON. And your name is Wood.

WOOD. Yes. I changed my name as she refuses to change hers, and won't marry me.

SIMON. In that case you're not Wood of Wundale.

WOOD. No, I'm Strapley - Strapley of Wundale. Known as Wanker Strapley. Now do you remember me?

SIMON. Strapley - Strapley, Wanker Strapley. No.

WOOD. Well, your brother certainly would. He was known as Armpits Hench. We were two of a kind, in that we were both considered drips - what was the Wundale word for drip?

SIMON. I really can't remember.

WOOD. It was 'plop'.

SIMON. Plop.

WOOD. Those of us who were called it are more likely to remember it than those of you who called us it. Plop. Yes, I'm a plop, Hench. Whom one can now define, after so many years ploppily lived as a chap who goes straight from masturbation to matrimony to monogamy.

SIMON. Oh, now there I think you're underestimating yourself. After all you have a wife, didn't you say, and now Joanna -

WOOD. I haven't got my wife any more. I doubt if I've got Joanna any more. But it's only appropriate that *you* should be the last common factor in our relationship. The first time I set eyes on her she reminded me of you.

SIMON. Where was that?

WOOD. At our local amateur theatricals. Joanna was playing in *The Winslow Boy.* She came on the stage in grey flannel bags, a white shirt and starched collar. She walked with a modest boy's gait, her eyes were wide with innocent knowledge. So did you walk down the Wundale Cloisters, that first year of yours. So I watched you then as I watched her. And there on my one side, were my two poor old sons, who've never reminded me of anyone but myself. And on the other, my poor old wife, the female plop, who from that second on ceased even to remind me that we shared a ploppy past. The years we'd spent together brooding over her mastoids, my haemorrhoids, and the mortgage on our maisonette, watching over our boys' sad little defeats, their failure to get into Wundale, their scrabbling for four O levels and then two A levels, their respective roles as twelfth man and scorer - they haven't even the competitiveness for sibling rivalry, poor old boys - all seemed, it all seemed such a waste, such a waste.

SIMON. But still you did succeed, to some extent at least, in breaking free. And you did succeed, to some extent I take it, with Joanna - so not altogether a case for predestination, when you think of it.

WOOD. Free meals, lots of gifts, little loans by the usual ploppy techniques of obligation and dependence - not that she felt dependent or obliged. She took what I offered and then asked for more. A generous nature. Did she get anything from you?

SIMON. She didn't ask for anything.

WOOD. Just as you never asked for anything from those boys - Higgens, Hornby, Darcy.

SIMON. It's true that Darcy was very kind with his tuck, but I hope I never took it as payment, nor did he offer it as such.

WOOD (*pause*). What was it like with Joanna?

SIMON. Well, it was, um, I'm sure you know - she's a very uninhibited um -

WOOD. It was, then, satisfactory?

SIMON. Well, as these things go.

WOOD. They don't for me. I'm incapacitated by devotion.

SIMON. But you live together?

WOOD. She allows me to share the flat I've leased for her. We have different rooms - I sometimes sit on the side of her bed when she's in it. More often when she's not.

SIMON. You're obviously in the grip of a passion almost Dante-esque in the purity of its hopelessness. You know, I really feel quite envious - for you every moment has its significance, however tortured, I just have to get by on my small pleasures and easy accommodations, my daily contentments -

WOOD. So she actually talks of me as a drip, does she?

SIMON. The ignorance of youth. Drips have neither your capacity for ironic self-castigation, nor more importantly your gift for the futile grand gesture.

WOOD. If she comes back, do you know what she'll do? She'll tell me about the boys she's slept with, the adults she's conned, the pot she's smoked. She'll tell me what a good time she had with you on your office floor -

SIMON. Sofa, actually.

WOOD. If she comes back. And I'll sit listening and yearning and just occasionally I'll soothe myself with the thought that one day she'll be dead, or even better old and unwanted and desperate - what I resent most about you, little Hench, is the way you seem to have gone on exactly as you promised you would at Wundale. If life catches up with everybody at the end, why hasn't it with you?

SIMON. But I haven't got to the end yet, thank God. I'm sure it will eventually.

WOOD. Sweet little Hench from Wundale, who picks off my Jo in an hour at his office, munches down a few pills, and then returns, without a worry in his head, the whole experience simply showered off, to his wife, who is doubtless quite attractive enough - is she?

SIMON. I find her quite attractive enough for me. Though taste in these matters -

WOOD. I'd like to kill you, Hench. Yes - kill you!

STEPHEN (*enters through the kitchen*). Si - (*Sees* WOOD.) Oh sorry, I didn't realise . . . Good God, it is, isn't it? Old Strapley, from Wundale?

WOOD. The name's Wood.

STEPHEN. Oh, sorry. You look rather like a chap who used to be at school with us, or rather me, in my year, Strapley.

WOOD. Really? What sort of chap was he?

STEPHEN. Oh actually, a bit of what we used to call a plop, wasn't he, Simon? So you're quite lucky not to be Strapley who almost certainly had a pretty rotten future before him. (*Laughs.*)

WOOD. Thank you for the sherry. (*Turns quickly, goes out.*)

SIMON. Not at all.

STEPHEN. I hope I haven't driven him off.

SIMON. Mmmm. Oh no, it's not you that's driven him off.

STEPHEN. What did he want?

SIMON. He was looking for somebody I once resembled. A case of mistaken identity, that's all.

STEPHEN. Well, if he had been Strapley, he'd hardly have changed at all, except that he's a quarter of a century older. Poor old Wanker Strapley. (*Sits down.*)

There is a pause.

Well Si, you were quite right, of course.

SIMON. Mmmm?

STEPHEN. I got it.

SIMON. Got what?

STEPHEN. The Assistant Headmastership.

SIMON. Oh. Oh good! (*Pause.*) Goody.

STEPHEN. You can imagine how stunned I was. I was so depressed when I got home, not only because I thought I'd lost the appointment, but because of that friend of yours -

SIMON. What friend?

STEPHEN. Golding. Jeff Golding. That he didn't even remember me, let alone what I'd threatened to do to him - and I could hear the children quarrelling in the garden, the baby crying in her cot, and when I sat down in the sitting-room there was a piece in *The Times* on the phasing out of public schools and private health, lumped together, and it all seemed - well! Then Teresa called out. I couldn't face her, you know how lowering her optimism can be - but I managed to drag myself into the kitchen - she had her back to me, at the oven, cooking up some nut cutlets for the childrens' lunch - and she said: 'Greetings, Assistant Headmaster of Amplesides.' Yes, Head-master's wife had phoned while I was here, isn't that ironic? I could hardly believe it. So. I crammed down a nut cutlet -

SIMON. What was it like?

STEPHEN. What?

SIMON. The nut cutlet.

STEPHEN. Oh, it was from one of Headmaster's wife's recipes. They're semi-vegetarian, you know.

SIMON. What did it *taste* like?

STEPHEN. Rather disgusting. But she's going to give us some more recipes if we like this one. Perhaps they'll be better.

SIMON. But you didn't like this one.

STEPHEN (*pause*). Aren't you pleased or even interested in my news?

SIMON. Of course I am.

STEPHEN. In spite of thinking MacDonald the better man? Well, you needn't worry about him, he's been offered a job too. As head of sixth form English.

SIMON. But you're head of sixth form English.

STEPHEN. Not any more. Headmaster reckons that with my new responsibilities I should step down from some of my teaching. I shall be head of fifth form English.

SIMON. Ah, fewer hours then.

STEPHEN. Actually more hours, but at fifth form level.

SIMON. Ah, less cerebration. That's even better. So - (*Loses thread, picks it up.*) so justice has been done to two excellent candidates.

STEPHEN. I shall still be senior to MacDonald, you know.

SIMON. Isn't his name MacGregor?

STEPHEN. Yes. (*Little pause.*) Thanks, Si. (*Ironically.*)

SIMON. What for?

STEPHEN. Sharing my triumph with me.

SIMON. Why don't you - have a drink.

STEPHEN. No, thank you. Headmaster's asked Teresa to ask me to look in after lunch for a celebration glass.

SIMON. Oh. Of what?

STEPHEN. Pansy wine, I expect, as that's their favourite tipple.

SIMON (*after a pause*). Do they make it themselves?

STEPHEN. Headmaster's wife's aunt's husband does.

SIMON. Does he? (*Little pause.*) What's it like?

STEPHEN. You know what it's like.

SIMON. No, I don't. What's it like?

STEPHEN. Why do you want to know what it's like?

SIMON. Because I can't imagine what it's like, I suppose.

STEPHEN. Oh yes you can. Oh yes you can.

> *Turns, goes out through the kitchen.* DAVE *enters left. He's slightly drunk. There is a pause.*

DAVE (*swaying slightly*). She's come. She's upstairs. She came all by herself.

SIMON. Who?

DAVE. That girl. Suzy. She dropped in for a cup of nescafe.

SIMON. That's very good news, Dave. But should you, now you've got her, leave her to have it all by herself. She sounds a highly-strung creature -

DAVE. Yeah, well the only thing is, I'm out of nescafe.

SIMON. Oh.

DAVE. Well, have you got any, man?

SIMON. No, I'm sorry, we don't drink it.

DAVE. Anything else?

SIMON. Nothing at all like nescafe, I'm afraid.

DAVE. What, no coffee at all?

SIMON. Oh yes, we've got coffee. But we use beans, a grinder, and a rather complicated filter process. Metal holders, paper cones -

DAVE. That'll do. Is it in the kitchen? (*He moves towards kitchen.*)

SIMON. Actually, it's rather a precious set.

DAVE. What? (*Returning.*)

SIMON. It's one of those few things I feel rather specially about.

DAVE. You mean you've got something against lending it to me?

SIMON. Not at all. The beans are in a sealed bag in an airtight tin -

DAVE. Oh yes you have. I can tell by your - your tone.

SIMON. My tone? Oh come now, Dave, that's only one possible gloss of my tone. No, you take the grinder, take the filters, the jug, the paper cones and the metal holders, and the coffee beans which come from a small shop in Holborn that keeps uncertain hours and can therefore be easily replaced with a great deal of difficulty, and don't addle your head with questions about my tone, good God! (*Pause.*) Go ahead. Please. (*Wearily.*)

DAVE. No thanks. No thank you! Because you do mind all right, you bloody mind all right.

SIMON. No, I don't.

DAVE. No, you don't, no, you don't bloody mind, do you - why should you, you've got it all already, haven't you? Machines for making coffee, a table covered with booze, crates of wine in your cellar, all the nosh you want, all the books you want, all the discs, the best hi-fi on the bloody market, taxis to work every morning, taxis home in the evening, a whole bloody house just for you and your sexy little wife - oh, you don't bloody mind anything you don't, what's there for you to mind, you shit you!

SIMON. Now that's not quite fair, Dave. It's not really a whole house, you know, since we converted the top floor at considerable expense and turned it over to you at an inconsiderable rent which you don't pay anyway. But then I don't mind that either.

DAVE. 'Course you bloody don't, why should you, you bloody like to run a pet, don't you, your very own special deserving case.

SIMON. I swear to you, Dave, I've never once thought of you as my pet or as a deserving case. If we'd wanted the former to occupy our upstairs flat we'd have got a monkey, and if we'd wanted the latter we'd have selected from among the unmarried mothers or the dispossessed old age pensioners. We thought quite hard about doing that, in fact.

DAVE. Then why didn't you?

SIMON. Because unmarried mothers mean babies, and babies mean nappies, and crying. While old age pensioners mean senility and eventual death.

DAVE. So I salve your bloody conscience without being a nuisance, eh? Right?

SIMON. Wrong. You salve my conscience by being a bloody nuisance. Your manners irritate me, your smell is unusually offensive, you're extremely boring, your sex-life is both depressing and disgusting, and you're a uniquely ungrateful cadge. But you really mustn't mind, because the point is that I don't, either. You have your one great value, that you run a poor third to recent births and imminent deaths.

DAVE. I'm not staying - I'm not staying - I'm not staying in the fucking top of your fucking house another fucking minute. You - you - (*Makes as if to hit* SIMON.)

SIMON *remains impassive.* DAVE *turns, goes out left. Noise of door slamming.* SIMON *closes door left. As he does so* STEPHEN *enters right.*

STEPHEN. It's sugary and tastes of onions. And it's quite revolting, just as you imagine.

SIMON. Well, I did imagine it would be revolting and probably sugary, but it never occurred to me it would taste of onions. But you can't have come back to report on its flavour already, you've only just left.

STEPHEN. I've been sitting in the car, thinking.

SIMON. What about?

STEPHEN. You, and your sneers. Oh, I don't altogether blame you, but I wish - (*Sits down, looks at* SIMON.) you'd had the guts to say it outright.

SIMON. Say what?

STEPHEN. That it's taken me twenty-four years to advance from Second Prefect of Wundale to Assistant Headmaster of Amplesides.

SIMON (*sitting down*). But that seems very respectable progress to me. At that rate you should make it to Eton, if it still exists, by your mid-fifties. And as that's what you want, why should I have a word to say against it?

STEPHEN. Nor against the way I'm doing it? My stuffing down nut cutlets, and herbal coffee and pansy wine. And then coming back for seconds.

SIMON. But you do rather more than eat the inedible and drink the undrinkable. You're among the best Junior Colts football managers in the country.

STEPHEN. You despise my job.

SIMON. You've a family to support.

STEPHEN. So you do despise my job, and despise me for doing it. Why don't you say it. That's all I'm asking you to do.

SIMON. But I don't want to say it! I can't remember when you were last as you've been today, or what I said then to make you feel any better. I wish I could, because that's what I'd like to say now.

STEPHEN. The last time I felt like this was eleven years ago, after Teresa had broken off our enegagement, and you didn't say anything to make me feel any better. What you did say was that I was well out of it.

SIMON. Well, as you've been back in it for eleven years, you'll agree that it has little relevance now.

STEPHEN. It had little relevance then, either. As I was desperately in love with her.

SIMON. Good God, all I probably meant, and I don't even remember saying it, was that if she didn't want to marry you then it was better to be out of it before the wedding.

STEPHEN. Oh no, oh no, all you meant was that *you* were relieved to be out of it.

SIMON. Out of what?

STEPHEN. Out of having for your sister-in-law a girl you thought tedious and unattractive. And still do. And still do.

SIMON. Look Stephen, this is really rather eccentric, even in the English fratricidal tradition. First you hold it against me that I won't join you in abusing yourself, and then you hold it against me that not only did I fail to abuse your intended wife eleven years ago, but won't join you in abusing her now that she is your wife and has borne you seven children -

STEPHEN. Six children.

SIMON. Nearly seven.

STEPHEN. Nearly six.

SIMON. Well, straight after the sixth, it'll be nearly seven. (*He gets up.*)

STEPHEN. Teresa's absolutely right about you. She always has been. You're just indifferent. Absolutely indifferent!

SIMON. In what sense? As a wine is indifferent, or prepositionally, as in, say, indifferent to -

STEPHEN. Imbeciles like Teresa. Go on, say it!

SIMON. But I don't want to say it.

STEPHEN. Not to me, no. But that's what you tell your clever-clever metropolitan Jeff Goldings, isn't it? That Teresa and I are imbeciles.

SIMON. I swear to you, Stephen, I've never told a soul.

STEPHEN. Answer me one question, Simon. *One* question! What have you got against having children?

SIMON. Well Steve, in the first place there isn't enough room. In the second place they seem to start by mucking up their parents' lives, and then go on in the third place to muck up their own. In the fourth place it doesn't seem right to bring them into a world like this in the fifth place and in the sixth place I don't like them very much in the first place. OK.

STEPHEN. And Beth? What about her?

SIMON (*after a little pause*). Beth and I have always known what we're doing, thank you Stephen.

STEPHEN. You think she's happy, do you?

SIMON. Yes, I do. And let's not let you say another word about her, because I don't want to hear it. Have you got that, Steve, *I don't want to hear it. (With low emphasis.)*

STEPHEN. No, I'm sure you don't. I'm sure you don't. The last thing you want to hear is how unhappy she is.

SIMON. Steve!

STEPHEN. Well, she is! So unhappy that last week she came around to Teresa and sobbed her heart out!

SIMON. Steve!

STEPHEN. She's having an affair, Simon. An affair with that Ned whom you so much despise. *That's* how unhappy your happy Beth is.

There is a long pause.

SIMON. With Ned. (*Pause.*) Beth's having an affair with Ned? (*Pause.*) Really? With Ned? Good God! (*Sits down.*)

STEPHEN. It's time you knew.

SIMON. No it isn't.

There is a pause.

STEPHEN. I had to tell you.

SIMON. Now that's a different matter.

There is the sound of a door opening left. BETH *enters.*

BETH. Hello. Hello, Stephen.

STEPHEN. Hello, Beth.

SIMON (*goes over, gives* BETH *a kiss*). You're back nice and early, aren't you?

BETH. Yes, I got an earlier train.

SIMON. Ah, that explains it. How was it, then, old Salisbury?

BETH. Old *Canterbury*, actually. Much as it ever was, except for the parts they've turned into new Canterbury.

SIMON. But the Cathedral's still there?

BETH. Although the French students were more interested in the new Marks and Spencers.

SIMON. And Ned?

BETH. Oh, he preferred the Cathedral.

STEPHEN. I really must be getting along. Headmaster will be wondering what's happening to me.

SIMON. Oh, but first you must tell Beth your news.

There is a slight pause.

The Assistant Headmastership, Steve.

STEPHEN. Oh. Oh yes. I got it.

BETH. Steve - how marvellous! (*Comes over, gives him a kiss.*) Congratulations - Teresa must be thrilled!

STEPHEN. Yes, she is. I've had some black moments since the
interview, but she was absolutely sure - and old Si jollied me
along a bit this morning. It's all a great relief, more than
anything. Well, I really must dash - see you both very soon -
(*Goes towards the kitchen door.*) Oh, by the way, Si - I was a
bit carried away just now, spoke a lot of nonsense, don't
know why I said it.

SIMON. Don't you?

STEPHEN. Yes, well I suppose I meant to hurt, but I didn't
mean harm, if you see.

SIMON. Well then that's fine, because no harm's been done. I
didn't take it seriously.

STEPHEN. Good. (*Hesitates, turns, goes out.*)

BETH. What did he say? (*Sits and lights a cigarette.*)

SIMON. Actually I could hardly make out - he was in a post-
success depression, I think, suddenly realising that what he's
got can therefore no longer be striven for. He'll be all right
the moment he sets his sights on a full Headmastership. Or
Amplesides is abolished. Triumph or disaster - you know, like
a drug. What about tea or coffee?

BETH. No, I've had some, thanks.

SIMON. Where?

BETH. On the train.

SIMON. Oh, then you're probably still trying to work out which
it was.

BETH. Did you enjoy your Wagner?

SIMON. I enjoyed some things about it, very much. The picture
on its cover for example, its glossy and circular blackness
when unsheathed, its light balance - and if the sound is any
good it'll be quite perfect.

BETH. You haven't managed to play it then?

SIMON. Very nearly, very nearly. But what with Dave and
Stephen, Jeff and Davina, the odd bod and sod, you know -

BETH. Oh, you poor thing, and you'd been looking forward to it
all week.

SIMON. Still, one mustn't snatch at one's pleasures, nor overplan them it seems. (*He puts the record away in its box.*)

BETH (*pause*). How was Jeff?

SIMON. Oh, in excellent form, really. He got drunk, threw his scotch in his girl's face, dashed off to Cambridge where he's been having it off with his ex-wife, Gwynyth. Did you know Gwynyth, or was she a little before your time?

BETH. Isn't it Gwendoline?

SIMON. Yes, yes, Gwendoline. Anyway, usual sort of Jeff saga, quite droll in its way.

BETH. And what's his girl like?

SIMON. She's got good tits and a nasty sense of humour.

BETH. And did she try to get you to bed?

SIMON. She did.

BETH. And how did you get out of it?

SIMON. Rudely, I'm afraid she's on to rather a good book, from the sound of it. Ah well -

BETH. Ah well, you can play your records now, can't you?

SIMON. Oh no. Wouldn't dream of it.

BETH. Why not?

SIMON. Well, for one thing, you hate Wagner.

BETH. Well, I'm going to have a bath.

SIMON. A four-hour bath?

BETH. Afterwards I've got to go along to the school - sort out the fares and docket them, that sort of thing.

SIMON. Ah! Well, in that case -

SIMON *moves to hi-fi and takes out record.* BETH *rises, hesitates, and moves towards him.*

BETH (*stops, looks at* SIMON). Stephen told you, didn't he?

SIMON. Mmmm? Told me what?

BETH. About me. At least I hope he has.

SIMON. Why?

BETH. So I shan't have to tell you myself.

SIMON. You don't have to.

BETH. What?

SIMON. Tell me.

BETH. What?

SIMON. Tell me anything you don't want to tell me. Stephen said nothing of significance about anything.

BETH. But you see, I may not want to tell you, but I do want you to know.

SIMON. Why?

BETH. Because there's an important problem we shall have to discuss. And I want you to understand. (*Sits on sofa.*)

SIMON. In my experience, the worst thing you can do to an important problem is discuss it. You know - (*Sitting down.*) - I really do think this whole business of non-communication is one of the more poignant fallacies of our zestfully over-explanatory age. Most of us understand as much as we need to without having to be told - except old Dave, of course, now I thought he had quite an effective system, a tribute really to the way in which even the lowest amongst us can put our education (or lack of it, in Dave's case) and intelli-gence (or lack of it, in Dave's case) to serving our needs. He's done really remarkably well out of taking the metaphors of courtesy literally, as for example when he asks, for a loan that is in fact and gift, and one replies, 'Of course, Dave, no trouble, pay it back when you can.' *But* this system com-pletely collapses when he's faced with a plainly literal reply, as for example when he asks to borrow our coffee set, and he's told that it'll be lent with reluctance and one would like him to be careful with it. Weird, isn't it, he can take one's courteous metaphors literally, but he can't take one's literals literally, he translates them into metaphors for insults, and plans, I'm reasonably happy to inform you, to move out at once. So I've managed one useful thing today, after all. When we come to think of his replacement, let's narrow our moral vision slightly, and settle for a pair of respectably married and out of date homosexuals who still think they've something to hide. They'll leave us entirely alone, and we can congratulate ourselves on doing them a good turn. We'll have to raise the rent to just this side of exorbitant of course, or they'll smell something fishy, but we'll pass the money straight on to charities for the aged, unmarried mothers, that sort of thing and no one need be the wiser, what do you think?

BETH. In other words, you do know.

SIMON. In other words, can't we confine ourselves to the other words.

BETH. What did Stephen tell you, please Simon.

SIMON. Nothing. Nothing, except for the odd detail, that I haven't known for a long time. So you see it's all right. Nothing's changed for the worst, though it might if we assume we have to talk about it.

BETH (*long pause*). How long have you known for?

SIMON. Oh - (*Sighs.*) about ten months it would be roughly. (*Pause.*) How long has it been going on for?

BETH. For about ten months, it would be. (*Pause.*) How did you know?

SIMON. There's no point, Beth -

BETH. Yes, there is. Yes, there is. How did you know?

SIMON. Well, frankly, your sudden habit, after years of admirable conversational economy on such day-to-day matters as what you'd done today, of becoming a trifle prolix.

BETH. You mean you knew I was having an affair because I became boring?

SIMON. No, no, over-detailed, that's all, darling. And quite naturally, as you were anxious to account for stretches of time in which you assumed I *would* be interested if I knew how you'd *actually* filled them, if you see, so you sweetly devoted considerable effort and paradoxically imaginative skill to rendering them - for my sake I know - totally uninteresting. My eyes may have been glazed but my heart was touched.

BETH. Thank you. And is that all you had to go on?

SIMON. Well, you have doubled your bath routine. Time was, you took one immediately before going out for the day. These last ten months you've taken one immediately on return too. (*Pause.*) And once or twice you've addressed me, when in the twilight zone, with an unfamiliar endearment.

BETH. What was it?

SIMON. Foxy. (*Little pause.*) At least, I took it to be an endearment. Is it?

BETH. Yes. I'm sorry.

SIMON. No, no, it's quite all right.

BETH. You haven't felt it's interfered with your sex-life then?

SIMON. On the contrary. *Quite* the contrary. In fact there seems to have been an increased intensity in your - (*Gestures.*) which I suppose in itself was something of a sign.

BETH. In what way?

SIMON. Well, guilt, would it be? A desire to make up -

BETH (*after a pause*). And did you know it was Ned, too?

SIMON. Ned *too*? Oh, did I also know it was Ned? No, that was the little detail I mentioned Stephen did provide. Ned. There I *was* surprised.

BETH. Why?

SIMON. Oh, I don't know. Perhaps because - well, no offence to Ned, whom I've *always* as you know thought of as a very engaging chap, in his way, no offence to *you* either, come to think of it, I'd just imagined when you did have an affair it would be with someone of more - more -

BETH. What?

SIMON. Consequence. *Overt* consequence.

BETH. He's of consequence to me.

SIMON. And *that's* what matters, quite.

BETH. What did you mean, when?

SIMON. Mmmm?

BETH. *When* I had an affair, you said.

SIMON. A grammatical slip, that's all. And since the hypothesis is now a fact -

BETH. But you used the emphatic form - when I *did* have an affair - which implies that you positively assumed I'd have an affair. Didn't you?

SIMON. Well, given your nature, darling, and the fact that so many people do have them these days, I can't see any reason for being bouleversé now that you're having one, even with Ned, can I put it that way?

BETH. Given what about my nature?

SIMON. It's marvellously responsive - warm, a warm, responsive nature. And then I realized once we'd taken the decision not to have children, - and the fact that you work every day and therefore meet chaps - and pretty exotic ones too, from lithe young Spanish counts to experienced Japanese businessmen - not forgetting old Ned himself - it was only realistic -

BETH. From boredom, you mean. You know I'm having an affair because I'm boring, and you assumed I'd have one from boredom. That's why I'm in love with Ned, is it?

SIMON. I'm absolutely prepared to think of Ned as a very, very lovable fellow. I'm sure *his* wife loves him, why shouldn't mine.

BETH. You are being astonishingly hurtful.

SIMON. I don't want to be, I don't want to be! That's why I tried to avoid this conversation, darling.

BETH. You'd like to go back, would you, to where I came in, and pretend that I'd simply caught the early train from Salisbury, and here I was, old unfaithful Beth, back home and about to take her bath, as usual?

SIMON. Yes, I'd love to. (*Little pause.*) I thought it was Canterbury.

BETH. It was neither. We spent the night in a hotel in Euston, and the morning in Ned's poky little office at the school, agonizing.

SIMON. Agonizing? Good God, did you really?

BETH. About whether we should give up everything to live together properly.

SIMON. Properly?

BETH. We want, you see, to be husband and wife to each other.

SIMON. Husband *and* wife to each other? Is Ned up to such double duty? And what did you decide?

BETH. Do you care?

SIMON. Yes.

BETH. His wife isn't well. She's been under psychiatric treatment for years. And his daughter is autistic.

SIMON. Oh. I'm sorry. I can quite see why he wants to leave them.

BETH. But I could still leave you.

SIMON. Yes.

BETH. But you don't think I will. Do you?

SIMON. No.

BETH. And why not?

SIMON. Because I hope you'd rather live with me than anybody else, except Ned of course. And I know you'd rather live with almost anyone than live alone.

BETH. You think I am that pathetic?

SIMON. I don't think it's pathetic. I'd rather live with you than anyone else, including Ned. And I don't want to live alone either.

BETH. But do you want to live at all?

SIMON. What?

BETH. As you hold such a deeply contemptuous view of human life. That's Ned's diagnosis of you.

SIMON. But the description of my symptoms came from you, did it?

BETH. He says you're one of those men who only give permission to little bits of life to get through to you. He says that while we may envy you your serenity, we should be revolted by the rot from which it stems. Your sanity is of the kind that causes people to go quietly mad around you.

SIMON. What an elegant paraphrase. Tell me, did you take notes?

BETH. I didn't have to. Every word rang true.

SIMON. But if it's all true, why do you need to keep referring it back to Ned?

BETH. It's a way of keeping in touch with him. If I forgot in the middle of a sentence that he's there and mine, I might begin to scream at you and claw at you and punch at you.

SIMON. But why should you want to do that?

BETH. Because I hate you.

The telephone rings. After the fourth ring, it stops. SIMON *makes a move towards it.*

SIMON. Oh, of course. I've put on the machine. (*Pause.*)

BETH (*quietly*). You know the most insulting thing, that you let me go on and on being unfaithful without altering your manner or your behaviour one - one - you don't care about me, or my being in love with somebody else, or my betraying you, good God! least of all that! But you do wish I hadn't actually *mentioned* it, because then we could have gone on, at least *you* could, pretending that everything was all right, no, not even pretending, as far as *you* were concerned, every-thing was all right, you probably still think it *is* all right - and - and - you've - you've - all those times we've made love, sometimes the very same evening as Ned and I - and yet you took me - in your usual considerate fashion, just as you take your third of a bottle of wine with dinner or your carefully measured brandy and your cigar after it, *and* enjoyed it all the more because I felt guilty, God help me *guilty* and so tried harder for your sake - and you *admit* that, no, not admit it, simply state it as if on the difference made by an extra voice or something in your bloody Wagner - don't you see, don't you see that makes you a freak! You're - you're - oh, damn! Damn. Damn you. (*Pause.*) Oh, damn.

There is a silence.

So you might as well listen to your Wagner.

SIMON. I must say you've quite warmed me up for it. And what are *you* going to do, have your cleansing bath?

BETH. No, go to Ned for a couple of hours.

SIMON. Oh dear, more agonizing in his poky little office. Or is that a euphemism for Ned's brand of love-play? Excuse me, but what precisely has all this been about? You complain of my reticence over the last ten months, but what good has all this exposition served, what's it been for Beth? Ned's not going to leave his wife, I don't want you to leave me, you don't even think you're going to leave me - we have a perfectly sensible arrangement, we are happy enough together you and I, insultingly so if you like but still happy. We could go on and on, with Ned, until you've gone off him, why,

why did you have to muck it up between you with your infantile agonizings.

BETH. Because there's a problem.

SIMON. What problem?

BETH. I'm going to have a baby.

SIMON (*stares at her for a long moment*). What? (*Another moment.*) Whose?

BETH. *That* is the problem. (*Goes out.*)

SIMON *sits in a state of shock.* DAVE *enters left.*

DAVE (*stands grinning at* SIMON). Well, I worked it out, you'll be unhappy to hear. Suzy put me onto you. She just laughed when I told her the stuff you'd said, she and her bloke had dealings with your type in their last place. You were trying to get me out, that's all. Well, it hasn't worked, see. I'm staying. See. And another thing, Suzy and her bloke are looking for a new place. I said they could move in upstairs with me. Got that? Got that? You won't like tangling with them either. (*Stares at* SIMON.) Having a bit of trouble sinking in, is it? (*Turns, goes out, leaving the door open.*)

SIMON *remains sitting, dazed. Then he goes to the drinks table, pours himself a small scotch. Looks at it. Frowns. Adds some more. Stands uncertainly, looks at the telephone, goes over to it. Remember something vaguely, presses the play-back machine.*

WOOD (*his voice*). Hello, Hench, Bernard Wood, né Strapley here. I expect by now my little visit has passed entirely out of your consciousness, it was all of an hour ago that I left, and you've no doubt had any number of amusing little things to engage your attention. Your life goes on its self-appointed way, as I sit in my empty flat, my home. I've taken off my jacket, and I've lowered my braces so that they dangle around me - a picture, you might say, of old Wood, né Strapley, quite abandoned at the last. Imagine it, the jacket off, the braces down, thinking of you as I speak into the tele-phone, clasped tightly in my left hand as my right brings up, not trembling too much - Hench - sweet little Hench - and point the gun at my forehead - no, through the - no, I can't do the mouth, the metal tastes too intimate - it'll have to be - picture it - picture it - and as I - as I - Hench, as I squeeze

- squee . . .

SIMON *switches off the machine, interrupting the message. He sits - motionless.*
JEFF *appears in the doorway left.*

SIMON (*sees him. Gets up slowly*). Ah yes. Jeff. Yes. All right, are we then? Get back to - (*Thinks.*) Oxford, did you?

JEFF. I didn't get to the bloody corner.

SIMON. Oh really. Why not?

JEFF. There was a police car, Simon, right behind me, then right beside me, then right on bloody top of me with the cops all bloody over me, breathalysing me, shaking me about, and then down at the station for the rest of it. That's why bloody not. And you tipped the buggers off, friend, Christ!

SIMON. What? (*Vaguely.*) What?

JEFF. No, don't deny it, don't deny it, please Christ don't deny it. Davina told me when I phoned her. She told me - you tipped them off. Christ!

SIMON. Oh. (*Thinks.*) That's what you believe, is it?

JEFF. That's what I bloody know, Simon.

SIMON (*calmly*). What sort of man do you think I am? (*He throws his scotch in* JEFF's *face.*) What sort of man do you think I am?

JEFF (*sputtering, gasping*). Christ, Christ! My eyes! My eyes!

SIMON *watches him a moment, then takes out his handkerchief, gives it to* JEFF.

Christ - (*Takes the handkerchief.*) Thanks. (*Little pause.*) Thanks. (*Little pause.*) Sorry. Sorry, Simon. (*Pause, goes and sits down.*) Can I have a drink? (*Pause.*) The bitch.

SIMON *hesitates, then goes and gets him a scotch, brings it to him.*

Thanks.

There is a pause.

Don't throw me out, eh? I've got nowhere to bloody go, and I don't want to go there yet.

SIMON. I'm going to play Parsifal. Do you mind?

JEFF. No, lovely. Lovely.

SIMON. You sure?

JEFF. Christ yes. You know I adore Wagner.

SIMON. No, I didn't know that.

JEFF. Christ, I introduced you. At Oxford. I bloody introduced you.

SIMON. Did you really(*Looks at him.*) Such a long time ago. Then I owe you more than I can say. Thank you, Jeff. (*Goes over to the hi-fi, puts on the record.*)

The opening bars of Parsifal *fill the theatre. They sit listening as the music swells.*
The light fades.

Curtain.

To Alan
for Ben, Simon, Peter and Charles

TWO SUNDAYS

TWO SUNDAYS was first presented by BBC Television on 23rd October 1975 with the following cast:

CHARLES	Alan Bates
PETER	Dinsdale Landen
ALISON	Rosemary Martin
HILARY	Georgina Hale
BOY	Steven Gover
BOWLER	Andrew Burleigh
HOUSE MASTER	Benjamin Whitrow
SCHOOL MASTER	Victor Langley
SCHOOL MASTER	Simon Cadell
CHILDREN	Paul Stencil
	Benjamin Bolger
	Daniel Bolger
	Amelia Bolger

Designed by Richard Henry
Directed by Michael Lindsay-Hogg
Produced by Kenith Trodd

1. Interior. Morning. BOWLER, *waking in the morning. Blinks, looks about him, makes a move to get out of bed.* Cut to:

2. Interior. Peter's bedroom. PETER *getting out of bed, looks and clearly feels dreadful.*

PETER. Oh Christ!

HILARY (*off*). Mmmmm?

PETER. It's eight thirty.

HILARY (*off*). Wah - ?

PETER. Eight thirty. (*Little pause.*) Eight thirty. (*Little pause.*)

HILARY (*off*). Mmmmm.

PETER. Shan't tell you the time again.

HILARY (*off*). Won't have to. I know. It's eight thirty.

PETER. But it won't be the next time you ask.

HILARY. Good.

PETER (*glares at her*). We've got a long bloody drive.

HILARY. I've got a long bloody drive. (*Off.*) You've got your usual bloody hangover.

   PETER *turns, goes out in his underwear and* cut to:

3. Exterior. CHARLES, *running across school playing-fields, in* long shot. *The sound of bells ringing, several boys walking, sitting. He comes closer and closer, his head swaying, eyes slightly glassy, breathing heavily until he's full in camera and*

then gone on past it. Hold *on the school playing-fields, and*
cut to:

4. Exterior. A school yard. *Different school, although this is not*
explicit. Several boys again, this time wearing school suits, in
some cases gowns, white shirts. Come in *on a* BOY *in a gown,*
sitting, reading.

BOY. Je suis le roi d'un pays pluvieux.

Sound of bells. He looks up, then around, as if looking for
someone. Then bends over his book. See him from a sudden
point of view *that turns out to be* BOWLER's. BOY *is*
smiling, as cut to:

5. Exterior. BOWLER, *from* BOY's point of view, *advancing*
towards him in grey flannels, white shirt, carrying cricket boots.
Gets to him.

BOY. Good morning then.

BOWLER. Hello.

BOY. Unusual togs for a Sunday morning.

BOWLER. They've put me down for a nine net.

BOY. I expect you'll enjoy that.

BOWLER. It's for the Junior Colts.

BOY. Gratters. (*Ironically.*) And luck.

BOWLER. We're fagging Rec. at break.

BOY. To Hell with all that.

BOWLER. We'd better go.

BOY *gets up, they move towards a building, slowly, and*
cut to:

6. Interior. Peter's and Hilary's kitchen. HILARY, *dressed, is*
drinking a cup of coffee, reading a paper. PETER *is leaning*
against the fridge door, dressed, drinking coffee, smoking. He
coughs slightly. HILARY *glances at him.*

PETER. Where's Jeremy?

HILARY. In the toilet.

PETER. The toilet!

HILARY. That's the word they use.

PETER. Who?

HILARY. Everyone in the Juniors, from the Headmistress down. They always say it.

PETER. Always? (*Going to the fridge.*) Lively conversationalists then. (*Opens the fridge door, takes out a bottle of wine.*)

HILARY. What's that?

PETER. Bottle of wine, isn't it?

HILARY. For breakfast?

PETER. For lunch. Last time they were on some herbal rubbish, I'm not risking that again. If he doesn't hurry, we won't make it for lunch. How can an illiterate spend so long on the lavatory?

HILARY (*calling*). Darling! Dar-ling!

And cut to:

7. Interior. Charles's study. *Still in his running shorts, etc; sweat dripping off him, is standing at his desk, one plimsolled foot on a chair, turning over the pages of a manuscript.*

ALISON (*off*). Are you in there?

CHARLES. Yes, darling. (*Listens, hand on a page.*)

ALISON's *footsteps off.* CHARLES *closes the manuscript, puts it unhurriedly away, as:*

ALISON (*at door, she is very pregnant*). They've started breakfast.

CHARLES. I'll just have a shower.

ALISON. Couldn't you after?

CHARLES. Oh, I pong fearfully.

ALISON. Well, we've got a lot to do, I haven't started the casserole . . . and I would like to tidy up . . .

CHARLES (*following her out*). Don't worry, darling, we'll cope.

Cut to:

8. Boy and Bowler, *walking down a passage. They stop.*

BOWLER. I thought we weren't allowed in Music until after prep.

BOY. No, it's all right on a Sunday.

BOWLER. You sure?

BOY. So I'll see you there after your nets. There's something I particularly want you to hear . . .

MASTER (*off*). Hey, you two, aren't you fagging recc.?

Cut to: MASTER, *at end of passage, not seen clearly, just a shape.*

BOY (*off*). Sir.

BOWLER (*off*). Sir.

MASTER. Come on then.

Seem to be coming in on him, instead come in on:

8A. Interior. Charles's and Alison's kitchen. *Three boys, aged eight, six, four, around the table. A girl, aged two, in a high chair; all eating.*

CHARLES. Well, we've got a jolly nice day in store for you chaps, haven't we, Mummy?

ALISON. A jolly nice day.

CHARLES (*sits down*). We must all be particularly nice to Jeremy, until he's used to us. He'll be the odd one out.

ONE OF THE BOYS (*off*). Don't like Jeremy.

CHARLES (*cheerfully*). You've forgotten him, it's been such a long time.

VOICE. But I remember I don't like him.

OTHER VOICE. Nor do I.

CHARLES. Then let's begin by pretending to like him, and if we practise hard, we'll end up by doing it.

9. Interior. Peter and Hilary in a car. PETER *is slumped down, smoking.* HILARY *is driving.* JEREMY *is in the back, strapped in.*

PETER. How did this come about, anyway?

HILARY. It was a conspiracy. The wife of your oldest friend invited the wife of his oldest friend and her husband, the oldest friend, to lunch. We wanted to ruin your Sunday.

PETER. You didn't have to accept.

HILARY. I had no choice. That's not true, I had a choice of any one of the next eight Sundays.

PETER. Then why didn't you choose the eighth?

HILARY. To avoid having this conversation then. (*Pause.*) It'll give Jeremy someone to play with, won't it, darling?

JEREMY (*off after a pause*). I hate them.

PETER. Then you, at least, shouldn't be too bored.

   Cut to:

10. Interior Charles's study. *He is putting the manuscript into a large brown envelope. Sound of car drawing up, opening and closing of doors, voices in greeting. Goes to the window, opens it, and as if from his point of view cut to:*

11. Exterior. *From point of view music room window, looking down over school yard. The yard is full of boys going off in different directions, walking together, separately, some standing in groups.* BOWLER *comes into picture, now dressed as* BOY, *only without the gown. He looks up, and cut to:*

12. Alison, Hilary, Jeremy, *other children, in the garden, and* PETER, *from his point of view looking up, sees* CHARLES, *who is smiling down. Cut to* PETER's *face, smiling slightly, and looking up, and cut up to:*

13. Music room window. BOY *at it, indistinct, looking down, seen from school yard,* BOWLER's point of view. *And* cut to:

14. Interior Charles's study. PETER *in it, lighting a cigarette, sighing, suddenly looks towards the door, as it begins to open. And* cut to:

15. Interior. *Music room door opens.* BOWLER *enters. He is dressed as in previous scene. He looks towards gramophone,* cut to: BOY, *just putting record on. He turns.*

BOY. It's to be Berg.

BOWLER. Oh.

> BOY *bends over gramophone.*
> BOWLER *sits down, adopts a listening posture.*
> BOY *fiddles with the gramophone, then as scraping noise of needle on the pre-music grooves, walks to sit down, and* cut to:

16. Interior. Charles's study. CHARLES *enters, carrying a quarter of a bottle of scotch and two glasses, one of which has a long drink in it.*

CHARLES. Sorry. I got it in specially and then forgot where I put it.

PETER. Very sweet of you.

CHARLES (*puts the full glass down on the desk, opens the bottle, makes as if to pour, stops*). You'd better look after yourself -

PETER. Thanks. (*Little pause.*) What are you drinking?

CHARLES (*little laugh*). Ribena, actually. I seem to have acquired an addiction to it - because of the children - well - (*Lifts his glass.*)

> PETER *has poured, lifts his, coughs slightly.*

CHARLES. Well - (*As if trying to think of something to say.*) Oh, there's something I wanted you to hear. It might amuse you - one of my sixth formers did it.

He goes over, turns on a tape-recorder, sits down.
PETER *makes an expression of bored irritation when*
CHARLES's *back is turned, sinks down, sips, smokes.*
CHARLES *sits down, as tape whirrs.*
There is a long silence.
There is a ping, followed by two more pings. Silence.
PETER *makes an expression. Sudden crashing of chords,*
and cut to:

17. Interior. Music room. *The climax of the Berg 78". The two*
boys sitting. The record stops. BOY *gets up, goes over, takes the*
record off, keeps his back to BOWLER. *Bends over to put the*
record back in its sleeve.

BOWLER (*after a pause, clears his throat*). It's jolly bloody good.

BOY (*looks at him*). Yes?

BOWLER. Well I liked it.

BOY. But did it make you laugh?

BOWLER. Laugh.

BOY. It's very and fantastically witty.

BOWLER. *You* didn't laugh.

BOY. Oh, I know all the jokes.

BOWLER. Then what did you put it on for?

BOY. Your entertainment, of course. And I wanted to con-
centrate on the grief, for once.

He puts on another record, walks back, scratching pre-music
begins, and cut to:

18. Interior Charles's study. PETER *sitting back, cigarette*
drooping from his lips, eyes half-closed as if in boredom, occa-
sionally wincing. See his face from CHARLES's *point of view,*
then his eyes taking CHARLES *in.* CHARLES, *from* PETER's
point of view, staring at him, looking away.
Through this, over, on the tape, lavatory flushing, dogs barking,
bird calls, savagely discordant violins. Then silence. Tape

whirring. A sudden girl's scream, terrible, from the tape.
Silence.
PETER *raises his eye-brows interrogatively.*

CHARLES. I'm not quite sure whether this is part of it. The
silence I mean. It goes on for twenty minutes. (*In a low
voice.*)

PETER. Oh. (*Short pause.*) May we not acknowledge it? Rather
than listen to it. Or whatever it is one does to silence.

CHARLES (*after another short pause*). Yes, yes, perhaps one
had better - I just wanted you to get a sense of its effect.
(*Gets up, goes over, bends for a moment.*) Once or twice I've
fancied I heard something *behind* the silence. But it's never
the same, so I suppose it must be imagination. (*Turns it off.*)
Perhaps that's what he intends. Well - (*Looks at* PETER
eagerly.)

PETER. A sixth-former, did you say?

CHARLES. Yes, but quite young. Just sixteen. A precocious lad.
I have hopes he'll pull off an Oxford place, at the very least.
He's utterly individual. I think I told you last time we had
quite a business coming to a policy on hair styles?

PETER (*clearly not remembering*). Oh yes.

CHARLES. And finally decided on a completely liberal view.
Well, you can imagine what we got - hair to the shoulders,
Afro-styles, the lot. (*Laughs.*) Except from young Tedhurst.
Young Tedhurst went bald.

PETER. Really? Disease or design?

CHARLES. Oh, design, I'm sure. And now this, for his Creative
Art's Project. Most boys wrote stories, or painted, or built
things, you know - but young Tedhurst - (*Gestures to the
tape-machine.*)

PETER. What will you say to him?

CHARLES. The truth of course. That I think it very, very
interesting.

PETER. Well, that should do the trick.

CHARLES. How do you mean?

PETER. That a bald, 16-year-old futuristic musician is entitled to exactly the same attention as any other boy.

CHARLES (*puzzled*). Well, of course he *is*.

PETER. Yes. (*Pause.*) Anyway, you're obviously still enjoying school, then.

CHARLES. Oh, yes. Last year they tried to promote me into more admin. and less teaching, but I wasn't having it. Those that can't aren't going to have *that* taken away from them. (*Smiles.*) By the way, did I mention to you, I've taken over the Junior Colts, soccer *and* cricket.

PETER. Really?

CHARLES. I thought that would surprise you.

PETER. For the exercise?

CHARLES. Partly. Of course I have to take further exercise to keep up with them. A run every morning before breakfast.

PETER. Christ!

CHARLES. I'm up to four miles.

PETER. Christ!

CHARLES. I really feel quite marvellous for it. (*Little pause.*) Well, how about you?

PETER. Oh, I'm not fit enough to take exercise.

CHARLES. But you're all right?

PETER. Yes. Oh yes thanks. Well, you know - (*Grunts vaguely.*)

CHARLES. And publishing? Anything changed? Last time you sounded a bit depressed -

PETER. Then nothing can have changed. I'm still editing the waste-products of immigrant intellectuals. We've just started a new paper-back series. Mind-formers of our time. Monographs on people like Marcuse, generally by people on whom we can do monographs in a few years time.

CHARLES. But you *were* very excited over a novel you'd received - a quite unexpected first novel, I think it was.

PETER. Was I? Oh yes - that got a few nice reviews. Nothing special happened - I suppose one or two people might have bought it.

CHARLES. But you're still doing novels, aren't you?

PETER. Now and then. We have to keep up a list, for appearances sakes. But of course with rising costs and declining literacy - (*Gestures.*)

CHARLES. Still, it's good that you are, for whatever reason. (*Pause.*) What about your own - you had one on the way, didn't you?

PETER. No. Rather yes, but no. Not any longer.

CHARLES. Don't say you've given it up?

PETER. I've already done my bit as publisher to add to the world's stock of unread books. I have no right to add to it as an author. (*Pause.*) Besides, it wasn't any good.

CHARLES. How do you know?

PETER. I assessed it in my second capacity, I decided it was probably worth more than a straight rejection, but that I wouldn't have recommended it for publication. In fact, I'd probably have taken the author out to lunch and gently discouraged him. Which is precisely what I did do. A bloody good lunch, too - oysters, Guinness and strawberries. Thus proving that I may be a poor novelist, but I'm a decent enough editor.

CHARLES. Still, it must have been, well, painful for you.

PETER. It was a relief, actually. I haven't the stamina to drink, smoke *and* write, in the evenings.

CHARLES. Well, perhaps it would be worth giving up, for something really important.

PETER. That's what I did.

CHARLES. Under the circumstances - (*Hesitates.*)

PETER. What?

CHARLES. Oh just something rather ironic. But it can wait. (*Pause.*) Well, the thing is - (*Stops, looks towards the door.*)

PETER *also looks towards to door, which is opening.* Cut to:

19. Interior. Music room. MASTER, *in a gown, standing at the door.* BOY *and* BOWLER, *on their feet as Mozart comes to an end on the gramophone.*

MASTER. Mysteriously Mozart from the other side of the door. While from the other side of the window something fashionably atonal. Berg?

BOY. Sir.

MASTER. When it shouldn't really be either, as you're both down to fag for seniors at Refec. Didn't you hear the Refec bells between the Berg and the Mozart?

BOY. Sir, we were just going, sir.

MASTER (*looks at them thoughtfully*). Good. By the way, isn't there some pettifogging regulation about the Music Room. *Is* one allowed to use it before six o'clock prep?

BOY *and* BOWLER *look at each other, seen from* MASTER's point of view.

BOY. We thought on Sunday, sir . . .

BOY *looks towards him, and as if we're going to see* MASTER *from his point of view. Cut to:*

20. Interior. Charles's study. ALISON, *the pregnant lady from the garden, at the door.*

ALISON. What are you two chaps up to? Lunch is ready, at least the children have all washed their hands, and Hilary's arranging them around the table,

PETER *is getting up.*

on which I'm just about to plonk the casserole, so if you're going to get up some of our brew, darling, you'd better nip about it sharpish.

CHARLES. Do you like home-made beer? I've been following that chap in *The Guardian*, sometimes it turns out all right.

ALISON. It's actually jolly delicious.

ALISON *holds the door open as first* PETER *then* CHARLES *pass, see them from her* point of view, *and then her eye going to the ash-tray containing* PETER's *stubs, and his glass and the scotch, as over:*

PETER. As a matter of fact, I did bring along a small contribution -

ALISON *makes a sardonic expression, closes the door, and* cut to:

21. Interior. *Sound of voices. School refectory.* **Come in on** *knives and forks plying between plates and mouths, then* cut to: BOY's *face, standing behind larger boys, who are eating. Then see him from the perspective of the* BOWLER, *also standing behind older boys, at a different table. There are other younger boys (clearly acting as fags) behind different tables.* BOY *smiles to* BOWLER, *then in response to an order from one of the older boys, moves to fetch a jug of water.* BOWLER *receives an order at the same time, comes back with bread, puts it down on the table, and* cut to:

22. Interior. Charles's kitchen. *An enormous table, around which the four boys from the garden are seated.* CHARLES, *behind the table, is on his feet and plonking bread down on the children's plates;* PETER *is moving around the other side, pouring out orange squash.* ALISON *is at the head of the table, serving casserole into bowls. Beside her, in a high-chair, is* NINDY, *the little girl.* HILARY *is seated, serving vegetables into the bowls. On the table several bottles of home-made beer, and two bottles of white wine. All this taken in fleetingly, then* cut to PETER's *face, sardonic, and then to* CHALRES, *intently the father.* CHARLES, *suddenly looks towards* PETER, *who smiles more intimately than in the study.* CHARLES *smiles back, while over:*

ALISON. Does Jeremy eat aubergines?

HILARY. He's worth trying, doesn't Nindy manage her fork well.

23. Exterior. School yard. *Lots of boys milling about, talking, then* come in on BOY's *face, as he and* BOWLER *slightly cut off from the others by a notice board.*

BOY. 'Gratters.

BOWLER. Oh, shut up!

BOY. I was only saying 'gratters, isn't that what chaps say to chaps when chaps get selected for the Junior Dolts.

BOWLER. Anyway, I'm only down because Duff is infirm.

BOY. Duff is infirm? But only mentally surely, not physically.

BOWLER. I mean, in in-firm, you know jolly well. I didn't select myself, you know, I was selected, you know. Surely you can understand that.

BOY. What?

BOWLER. That it's not my fault.

BOY. What's not our fault?

BOWLER. If I happen to get selected because I was bowling off-spins in the nets, I didn't know I could bowl off-spin even, so it's not my fault, is it?

BOY. But it's your fault when you smirk about it.

BOWLER. I'm not smirking! (*Turning around on him.*)

BOY. No, it's quite true, you're not. Coming for a walk?

BOWLER. No.

BOY. Why not?

BOWLER. Because I can't.

BOY. Why can't you?

BOWLER. Because I'm meant to be playing, that's why.

BOY. But your match isn't until Thursday, it said on Notice.

BOWLER. It's squash, this afternoon.

BOY. Oh, squash!

BOWLER. It's the House Shield semi-finals.

BOY. 'Gratters!

    Cut to:

24. Exterior. Charles's garden. CHARLES *and the four boys are playing soccer on the lawn. See them from* PETER's *point of view. Then take in* PETER, *watching them. He is sitting in a deck chair at the end of the garden with a bottle of wine at his side, a cigarette in one hand, a glass in the other. He looks up suddenly,* *and to his right, at the approach of* HILARY, *not yet seen, and* cut to:

25. Interior. Spectators' balcony, squash courts. Come in *on* MASTER's *face, looking down, as* off, *in the same court,* BOWLER's *voice:*

BOWLER (*off*). Oh, jolly good serve.

Sound of rallies punctuates the conversation.

MASTER. Some verse?

Cut to:

BOY (*with an exercise book open on his knees, a pencil in his hand*). Sir.

MASTER. Why here?

BOY. Well, supporting House too, sir. It's the House Shield semi-finals.

MASTER. Ah, well that's very keen of you. Let's hear a mite of applause then.

BOY. He hasn't done anything to applaud yet, sir, he's behind love - four.

BOWLER (*off*). Jolly good serve.

BOY. Five love.

MASTER. Then you must applaud his opponent. That's the done thing, isn't it?

BOY. Sir.

MASTER. Then kindly do it.

BOWLER (*off*). Jolly good serve!

BOY *applauds, and on him clapping and looking first down, into the court, then up again, as if at* MASTER, *see, as if from his* point of view *but* cutting to:

26. Exterior. Garden. HILARY's *face, from* PETER's *point of view, their voices carefully lowered, as* over, *the sound of* CHARLES, *shouting encouragement.*

HILARY. You might show willing.

PETER. But I'm not.

HILARY. It's a little embarrassing for Jeremy, though, *his* father not playing.

PETER. It would be more embarrassing for him if I did. He hates football too.

HILARY. But at least he's joining in.

CHARLES (*off*). Oh, hard cheese, Jeremy.

PETER. Poor little sod had no option.

HILARY. Well, I must say, you present a very pretty spectacle -

ALISON (*off, advancing*). I say, would you mind looking?

PETER. What?

HILARY (*looking down*). O well done, Nindy.

PETER *looks down, on his face a sudden grimace.*

HILARY (*under her breath*). Say something! (*Aloud.*) Marvellous darling!

PETER. Yes, brilliant.

Cut to: *The little girl, holding chamber pot for inspection.*

ALISON (*behind*). Isn't she a clever girl! (*Claps.*)

HILARY *also claps.* PETER *also claps.*

ALISON. Daddy, Daddy, Nindy's done a lovely little jobs for Pete, right into her pottie!

CHARLES (*bounds up, sweat running down his face, breathing deeply*). What a clever girlie. (*Claps, and sinks exhausted to the porch.*)

PETER (*sotto voce, to* HILARY). What do they do when she does a lovely big jobs?

HILARY *lets out a laugh, suppresses it, turns, moves off after* ALISON *who is leading* NINDY, *carrying the pot, away. From the garden, noises of game continue.*
CHARLES *sits recuperating, seen from* PETER's *point of view then* cut to:

PETER. You seem a bit done in for a chap who's up to four miles and the Junior Colts.

CHARLES (*over*). It's the heat. (*Panting.*)

Cut *as if back to* CHARLES, *and instead, to:*

27. Interior. School showers. BOWLER *is sitting beneath the clothes peg on a bench opposite the showers. He is stripped down to his shorts, and is taking off his socks. He sniffs at them in fascinated disgust, drops them to the floor, looks up, as* voice over:

BOY. Hard luck.

Cut *to him as he enters, stands uncertainly.*

BOWLER. I pong.

BOY *comes over, sits down on the bench beside him.*

BOWLER. I don't know how you can sit there.

BOY. Why not?

BOWLER. Because I pong.

BOY. That's because you've been running about, losing.

BOWLER (*gets up, takes off his shorts, goes to the shower*). I wouldn't have, if you hadn't been there.

BOY. Run about?

BOWLER. Lost! You put me off.

BOY. But it doesn't matter, you losing. Master told me so.

BOWLER *looks at him, goes under the shower and* cut to:

28. Interior. Charles's bathroom. CHARLES *drying his face. He finishes, stares ahead, makes a face as if reaching a decision. Puts the towel back, and* cut to:

29. Interior. Charles's study. PETER *is staring blankly ahead, hand around a glass; cigarette in his other hand. Suddenly sighs, as if with boredom. Coughs slightly.*

30. Interior. Showers. BOY *is still sitting, staring down.* Cut to:

BOWLER *sitting opposite him, towel around his waist, putting on socks. As he does so, glances furtively at* BOY. *Glances away. Draw the* camera back, *to take in the two of them. Then* cut to:

31. Interior. Charles's study. CHARLES, *full face. He is closing the door, looks at* PETER. *Take in the two of them,* PETER *making a small effort at a greeting.* CHARLES *turns away. Camera on him. His face, for a second, desperate. Turns around, looks at* PETER.

CHARLES. Sorry.

PETER. What? What for?

CHARLES. All this. Family casseroles, soccer on the lawn, home-made beer. You must hate it.

PETER. Of course, I don't.

CHARLES (*smiles*). It's the only way Alison knows of doing things.

PETER. It's a splendid way. Besides, don't forget I didn't drink the beer or play soccer and the casserole was delicious. And so was the home-made bread.

CHARLES. The beer's really not at all bad.

PETER. Look, why don't we meet in town for lunch some time.

CHARLES. We always decide to do that.

PETER. Nothing could be easier to arrange.

CHARLES. Fine.

There is a pause.

PETER. I'll give you a ring early in the week, just as soon as I've checked on my office diary -

CHARLES. Right. (*Little pause.*) One gets such odd fragments of information, doesn't one? From each other. But usually not the sequels.

PETER. Yes. It's very - tantalising.

CHARLES. I mean, I take it everything's all right, to do with that girl -

PETER. Girl?

CHARLES. The one you were having an affair with.

PETER. Oh. Oh yes. (*Little pause.*) Which one was that?

CHARLES. The Australian.

PETER. Ah, yes. Long gone. All the way back to Australia, thank God! That was a long time ago.

CHARLES. You were worried that Hilary might find out, you thought she'd make trouble.

PETER. Hilary?

CHARLES. No, the Australian.

PETER. That's right. Yes, yes, she did go through a period of Antipodean bluster. I think she just wanted to liven me up a bit. She found me boring, when it came to it. She had some idea that adultery should be, well, more spectacular, especially in the literary world. At least a few *éclaircissements*.

CHARLES. Anyway, Hilary never did find out?

PETER. Christ no. She wouldn't really have done anything underhand - she was all right. She was quite nice actually. Her book's done quite well, too, considering it came at the tail end of all that business. Have you read it?

CHARLES *shakes his head.*

In the Afterword, which she had stuck in afterwards, so to speak, there's an account of an affair she had with a married chap who used to bring a spare pair of knickers to her flat in his briefcase. That was me. Hilary thought it was funny.

CHARLES. That it was you?

PETER. No, no - just the description. She read it out to me, bits of it, of course she hadn't the least idea -

CHARLES. Good God, what did you do?

PETER. I laughed too. It struck me as really quite exceptional, to lie in bed listening to one's wife innocently reading out an account of one's adultery . . .

CHARLES. Yes, I can see . . . (*Laughs.*) Anyway, that's all over.

PETER. Mmmm. Yes.

There is a pause.

CHARLES. I remember your saying that if you got out of *that* one intact you'd make sure there'd never be another.

PETER. Did I say that?

CHARLES. Don't you remember?

PETER. Well, there have been so many since . . .

CHARLES. You mean now?

PETER. Not really, no. Well, one of the editor's secretaries . . . she's worse than me. She keeps a supply of VD pills in her bag, makes me take them . . . Extremely organised. Oddly enough, I hear she's not a very good secretary.

CHARLES. Where do you do it?

PETER. Mmmm? (*Slightly shocked.*)

CHARLES. No, I was just curious. Sorry.

PETER. No, it's all right. In my office, at lunch-time, or after hours - when she's not going on somewhere more interesting and I don't have to get home for anything.

CHARLES. But isn't that risky?

PETER. Not really. I lock the door and leave the key in -

CHARLES. Surely people suspect.

PETER. I imagine there are the usual jokes. But as long as they don't reach Hilary - (*Pause.*) The most depressing thing, you know, *the* most depressing thing, is that I used to feel a certain amount of post-coital tristesse. Well, guilt. But these days I can scarcely be bothered to feel shifty when I get home. Extra-marital sex is as over-rated as pre-marital sex. And marital sex, come to think of it.

CHARLES. Then why do you have it?

PETER (*sighs*). I don't know. Well, the first time is still quite fun, it's having to go on and on.

CHARLES. Why do you?

PETER. From politeness. I mean, one can't just have it off, tip one's hat . . .

CHARLES. But you still love Hilary, don't you?

PETER. What?

CHARLES. Hilary.

PETER. What?

CHARLES (*after a long pause*). Love Hilary.

PETER. Christ! (*Pause.*) Of course I do. (*Pause.*) There's not a
day at the office, when the telephone rings, not a day when
at least once (*Pause.*) I don't have a spasm of terror, and
think: 'Not this time, please let nothing have happened to
her this time. Or Jeremy.' You know. I'm frightened for
them. I want to die before they do so at least I shan't spend
my last years - first me, and then Hilary, and then after a long
intermission - Jeremy. That seems only fair, except that I
know that life doesn't work on fair principles, which are
anyway formulated by types like me in Greenwich . . . Who
knows? Who knows what . . . I'm frightened for them.
(*Pause.*) I know she is for me. (*Pause.*) Christ, that's a
marriage, isn't it? (*Pause.*) Bloody Hell, of course I love . . .
(*There is a pause.*) What do you mean?

CHARLES *gets up, walks restlessly around the room.*
PETER *watches him, then loses interest, concentrates on his
drink.*

CHARLES. There's something . . . (*Stops.*)

PETER (*not paying attention*). Mmmm?

CHARLES. The irony is . . . (*Looks at* PETER, *then turns, opens
the drawer of his desk, takes out a bulky, and large, brown
envelope.*) Look.

CHARLES *hesitates, then, making up his mind carries it over
to* PETER, *hands it to him. Cut as if to* PETER's *face, but
instead to:*

32. Interior. The showers. In *on* BOWLER's *face. He is now
dressed and holding a sheet of paper.* BOY *is standing, turned
away from him.*

BOWLER. About me?

BOY. That's right. Didn't you recognise yourself, I thought you
would as it's so complimentary.

BOWLER. Well, I can't . . . I've only read it once. (*Little pause,*

looks down, tries to read it again.) It's difficult, with you
sitting there - well, you, I mean you just stick it in my hand -

BOY. I'm putting you off again, am I? You can't win at games
when I'm watching you can't read when I'm watching -

BOWLER. Why don't you stop watching then?

BOY. You like being watched.

BOWLER. Rubbish, what bloody rubbish! It's a lousy poem, it's
just bloody rubbish!

BOY (*trying to control a shaking voice*). I'm glad I showed it to
you. I was sure I'd get an intelligent assessment.

BOWLER. They're right about you, what they say, you're just a
pseudo, really, loping about listening to music and scribbling
poems and not doing anything at all.

BOY (*his voice now shaking*). The irony is that I thought you
might have a touch of intelligence. The irony is that you're
an extremely stupid sort of little person. The irony is I've
been wasting my time on you.

BOWLER (*shouting*). Then why don't you leave me alone?

BOY (*shouting*). Yes, why don't I?

They stare at each other.
Over the end of this scene.

CHARLES (*shouting*). That's enough, boys. Either play sportingly,
or don't play at all. Don't forget, it's only a game.

Cut to:

33. Interior. Charles's study. In *on* PETER *looking down at the
envelope in his lap. He picks it up surreptitiously, as if weighing
it, also tests its bulk with his thumbs. A general sense of his
being aghast. Then looks towards* CHARLES, *and from his*
point of view.

CHARLES (*leaning out of the window*). Ali darling, do you
want me to come down . . . ?

ALISON, off, *in the garden, voice not audible.*

CHARLES. Jolly good, thanks, darling. (*Straightens from the
window, closes it, pauses staring out, then turns. Looks*

towards PETER.) I was going through one of those passages
that one goes through, you know, feeling a bit desperate, not
sure I could go on - (*Gestures.*) then one day, just after I'd
got back from my run I just - sat myself down and began it.
I didn't intend it to come out as a full-length novel, I had no
idea.

PETER. Well, these things happen.

CHARLES. Even now I can scarcely believe I've finished it. Or
whether what I've finished is something *there*, you know,
created. Or therapy. (*Little pause.*) I expect you'll be able to
tell me, no punches pulled. (*Smiles.*)

PETER *smiles.*

CHARLES. What I do know is that it in a sense saved my
life.

PETER. Well, that's certainly to its credit. Has anyone else read
it?

CHARLES. No.

PETER. What does Alison feel about it?

CHARLES. Actually, she hasn't read it either. In fact, I'd better
warn you - mm, she doesn't even know I've written it. Oh,
she knows I've been working on something, of course, but
I've rather let her go on thinking that it's the Molière trans-
lations, you know, the ones I started just after we came
down. (*Pause.*) Actually, I'd rather she didn't know, well, at
least just yet. You'll be able to help me there, too. You see,
it's about us?

PETER. Us?

CHARLES. Well, our marriage. (*Stares at him.*) It's *not*, of
course, but there are certain - well, I wouldn't want Alison
to think it *was* about us, is perhaps the best way of putting
it. There are inevitable similarities - especially between
myself and the central chap. There's a chap who's a little
like you in it too, only superficially - For one thing, he
commits suicide.

PETER. Well, there at least he's a little unlike me. If only
superficially.

CHARLES. No, no. I meant the other chap.

PETER. Oh, the chap a little like you?

CHARLES. Mmmm.

PETER. Can you tell me why, or would that ruin the suspense?

CHARLES. No, no. As he commits suicide on the first page. And the last.

PETER. He does it twice?

CHARLES. No, it's the same suicide. The structure is complex. Circular. But I hope organic. (*Pause.*) He commits suicide because he's unhappy really, that's what it comes to. In his work and his well, marriage. That's the part of it that Alison might not understand - the difference between autobiography and fiction.

PETER. It's frequently muddling.

CHARLES. Well, not for you - you'll know at once - his attitude to the children, for example, his wife's pregnancies - and various things that he does or feels at work -

PETER. What work does he do?

CHARLES. He's a teacher. A public school teacher. Not very imaginative that, I know, but in his real self he's so different from myself -

PETER. Anyway, *your* real self.

CHARLES. Exactly. Yes. Look - there is *one* thing - one section that I would like to clarify - where something's said, explicitly said, about his feeling for one of the boys. His sense of torture, and the way in which the word desire is used - (*Painful pause.*) well, that *is* - (*Hesitates.*) You'll understand. You'll understand. And also about friendship - there's a passage, a meditation - he thinks about his most important relationship and the tone of the passage is - well, intended to be - acerbic.

PETER (*after a pause*). Don't worry, I'll read it as a novel.

CHARLES. I know. But I can't help feeling a little treacherous. In the sense that you meant years ago, when you first started being, mm, unfaithful - you said that for you the real treachery wasn't what you did with another woman, it was what you said to her about your wife.

PETER. Did I say that?

CHARLES. Anyway that's the sense in which I feel treacherous. Towards Alison. As if I had betrayed a deep confidence -

PETER. On that analogy, you haven't, yet. Not until I've read it - or somebody else has. Perhaps you ought to reconsider letting me see it.

CHARLES. No, no. You must read it.

PETER. But only if you're sure -

CHARLES. The treachery is finding it out. I can't go back on that. The truth is that it's all there. It's no good my fooling myself or trying to fool you, of all people. You'll know. It's all there.

PETER (*after a pause*). Yes, well it usually is. (*Smiles.*)

CHARLES. How do you mean?

PETER. In a first novel.

CHARLES. If it hadn't been for you, I wouldn't have written it. You're the one -

Bring them both in camera, drawing back slightly, looking towards each other.

CHARLES. To whom I've always privately addressed my most private feelings. Some friendships endure as what they were even though they *are*. No longer. What they were. Isn't that true? Isn't it the same for you?

Hold on the two of them, sitting in silence, for as long as possible. Then one beat longer than that, as fade into:

34. Interior. The showers. BOY *is sitting staring straight ahead.* BOWLER *is sitting opposite, staring down. He looks at* BOY.

BOWLER. Are you all right?

BOY remains immobile, staring blankly.
BOWLER gets up, goes over to him slowly, apprehensively, hesitates, sits down beside him, clears his throat.

Are you?

They sit in misery.
Fade to:

35. Interior. Charles's study. *As before.*

PETER (*suddenly coughs, clears his throat*). I'm sorry.

CHARLES. Why?

PETER. Well, I hadn't realised you were un - well, unhappy.

CHARLES. Oh, I'm sure I'm not. Any more than anybody else, anyway. I'd be far more unhappy if Alison found out - well, aren't *you* unhappy?

PETER: Mmm, well - (*Coughs slightly and fade to:*)

36. Interior. Showers. *The boys as before.*

BOWLER (*after a pause*). Well, liking me so much. (*In a mutter.*)

BOY. Because you've stopped liking me? (*Very low.*)

BOWLER (*in a mutter*). No, well - it's not that, it's - (*Shrugs.*)

BOY. You don't like me any more.

BOWLER. Yes, I do. (*Embarrassed.*)

BOY. How do you know I like you?

BOWLER. Well, if you don't - I mean -

BOY. Why don't you go?

BOWLER. What will you do?

BOY. Stay here.

BOWLER. What for?

BOY *doesn't answer.*

Well, for how long?

BOY. Until I get up.

BOWLER. The Refec bell's gone. (*Pause.*) We're still on Fag. (*Pause.*) Come on! (*Pause.*) We better go.

BOY *continues to sit.*

BOWLER. Well - Well, I'm jolly well - (*Gets up, stands indecisively.*)

BOY. You're very stupid.

BOWLER *still indecisive, takes* BOY's *arm, tries to pull* BOY

up. BOY *resists passively, until he's hauled up, then begins to resist violently, pushing* BOWLER *away, in a sudden, un-expected burst of violence.*
They stand staring at each other.
Sounds off, of a door opening and closing. They swing their heads in alarm, left and cut to:

37. Interior. Charles's study. ALISON *is standing at the door,* NINDY *in her arms.*

PETER. Ah, is she? I'll be right down. (*Getting up.*)

ALISON. I'll dig Jeremy out of the cellar.

CHARLES. Aren't you staying for tea?

ALISON (*who has turned away, turns back, briefly*). It's rather a long drive, Hilary feels.

CHARLES. Oh. (*Getting up.*)

   ALISON *goes off.*

CHARLES (*as* PETER *drains off the rest of his drink, stubs out his cigarette*). We were just beginning to talk. Naturally.

PETER. It is a long drive and Jeremy gets tired - (*Moves towards the door.*)

   CHARLES *picks up the envelope, hands it to* PETER, *who has left it on the floor.*

PETER. Ah!

   PETER *takes it, slips it under his arm,* CHARLES *holds the door open for him and as he passes, suddenly puts his hand on* PETER's *arm.* PETER *turns, looks at him.* CHARLES *smiles.* PETER *smiles back, slightly awkwardly, they go out, leaving the door open, and* fade *the open door into:*

38. Interior. Master's study. *A light, airy, and civilised place.* Fading in *on the open door, seen from* MASTER's *point of view from his desk. He is not yet seen, nor his room, just the open door, through which* BOWLER *and* BOY *enter, self-consciously. They stand in the room,* MASTER *comes into* camera, *but his face* out of camera, *passes the two boys, closes the door, turns,* *passes back. Sits down. His face coming into* camera *as he does so.* Cut *as if to the two boys,* come in on:

39. Interior. Charles's hall. *Front door open.* PETER *and* CHARLES *standing at it. From behind, up the stairs, the cries of children, sound of bath-water running,* ALISON's *voice.*

ALISON (*off*). Don't turn on the tap! Leave the taps alone!

PETER. I'll give you a ring -

    Off *sound of car honking.*

    Ah, there they are - Well, I'll give you a ring.

CHARLES. At the school. (*Low.*)

PETER. Right.

    ALISON *comes down, stands beside* CHARLES *as* PETER *moves outside.*

ALISON. I was going to fix something up with Hilary, tell her I'll give her a ring.

PETER. Right, and thanks for a lovely - (*Gestures. He doesn't have the envelope in his hand.*)

ALISON. No, it was lovely -

CHARLES. Yes.

PETER. Well -

    Stay *on* CHARLES *and* ALISON *staring out from the hall, saluting as* off:
    The sound of the car honking farewells.
    The door closes. Cut back *into the hall.* ALISON *is going up the stairs,* CHARLES *is standing in the hall, looks down, sees in the pram the envelope.* Come in *on his face as he picks it up.*

ALISON. He's certainly putting it on, isn't he?

CHARLES. What? Who?

ALISON. Surely you noticed? His face is quite -

    A ring at the doorbell. CHARLES *opens the door on* PETER.

PETER. Christ, I nearly forgot, I thought I had it in my hand. I put it - (*Looks vaguely around.*)

CHARLES *holds it out to him.*

ALISON (*over*). Forgotten something?

PETER. No, got it thanks. 'Bye. 'Bye. (*The second to* CHARLES.)

CHARLES *closes the door.*

ALISON (*over*). What was it?

CHARLES. Oh just some cigarettes or something -

ALISON (*over*). Can you check in the bathroom, I'm doing Ophelia. They're meant to be washing their hands but they're mucking about with the bath-taps -

CHARLES *during this, goes up the stairs, heavily, rather tired. Camera stays with him as he opens bathroom door, then cut to his face, as if from within the bathroom, from which splashes and shouts have been coming. Just for a second an expression of collapse, then a smile, and in pleasantly jocular tones.*

CHARLES. What do you boys think you're doing? You're supposed to be washing your hands.

Cut instantly to:

40. Interior. Master's study. In *on his face, friendly and slightly satirical.*

MASTER. . . . all over the school. Mr Jameson finds you in the Music Room when you should be fagging at Rec., M. Fouce wonders why you always sit in the back of the class and whisper passionately over Baudelaire, he thinks, when you ought to be translating *Le Malade Imaginaire,* and Mr Jameson stumbles across you in Change, when you should be fagging in Rec. Mmm?

BOWLER/BOY (*after a pause*). Sir.

MASTER. How's your chest?

BOY. I've still got asthma a bit, sir.

MASTER. You're still chitted for all games then?

BOY. Sir.

MASTER. How did the Shield match go?

BOWLER. Oh - oh all right, sir.

MASTER. You won then?

BOWLER. No, sir.

MASTER. Really. What they call in sporting circles a bit of an upset?

BOWLER (*stammeringly*). Not really, sir, I mean I didn't mind too much . . .

MASTER. Mmmm. (*Looks at* BOWLER, *see* MASTER's *face from* BOWLER's *point of view. Smiles.*) Well, I've really got nothing more to say to you than this. If you're going to be caught in the wrong places at the wrong times, could you contrive to do so separately?

BOWLER. Sir.

BOY. Sir. But it's all right to be in the Music Room together at the right time, and other places at the right time?

MASTER (*after a short pause*). There is no school regulation to prevent boys from being friends. As you're in the same House and the same Form there isn't even convention to hold you back. (*Pause.*) I'd like a word with each of you privately, if I may. Why don't you run along to Matron and get your next week's chit, and then come back . . .

BOY. Sir.

BOY *turns, goes out, as he closes the door, see from his* point of view MASTER *and* BOWLER, *then* cut to MASTER's *face, as behind, sound of door closing.*

MASTER. You *are* friends, are you?

BOWLER (*after a pause*). Sir.

MASTER. What sort of friends are you?

Cut to *his face, looking towards* BOWLER, *solicitously, then* cut *as if to* BOWLER, *and come in on:*

41. Interior. The car. HILARY *driving*, JEREMY *strapped in behind*, PETER *beside* HILARY, *leaning back, eyes closed,* *cigarette between lips.* In *on his face:*

PETER. I suppose so. But he's, let's face it, one of those friends
   - (*Lets the sentence trail away.*)

HILARY. I wish you'd finish that sentence.

PETER. Oh, just that one can't bear seeing.

HILARY. Then why do we go on seeing them?

PETER. We scarcely do any more. Besides, *you* accepted. (*Pause.*)
   I was prepared for a ghastly day -

HILARY. Very well prepared, with your bottles of wine and
   cigarettes in every pocket -

PETER. But not sufficiently prepared for this? (*Beats the envelope
   with his hand.*) Christ, a bloody novel!

HILARY. You might like it.

PETER. Yes. (*Gives a half-laugh.*) That'd be a blow.

HILARY. To whom?

PETER. To me, of course. He had his purple passage at school,
   he doesn't deserve another go now I've settled him down as
   a successful failure.

HILARY. What an appalling thing to say. (*Pause.*) Besides, you
   used to claim he was very talented - in those days when you
   wanted to make your friends sound glamorous and mysterious.
   At least to me.

PETER. That was a long time ago, and even then I was going a
   long way back. When it was assumed we'd both of us go a
   long way.

HILARY (*after a pause*). Well then, let's hope it's terrible. You
   can still make appropriate noises.

PETER. What are the appropriate noises for not wanting to
   publish it?

HILARY. Oh. Is that what he's after? (*Looks at* PETER.) You
   poor old sod.

   Cut to:

42. Interior. Master's study. BOWLER *is now sitting, in a chair.*

MASTER *on the edge of the desk, talking in a low, confidential voice.*

MASTER. . . . after all be a reason for choosing him among so many. You see, your interests are very different, or so it seems to an uninvolved eye. Aren't they?

BOWLER. Sir.

MASTER. I mean no reflection on your academic standing, you work as hard as can be expected from someone with so many obligations, in the squash courts, the cricket fields - I gather you've developed an off-spin of some consequence. (*Smiles.*) So. I'm fairly confident that your general all-roundedness will stand you in some stead when you come to think between Oxford and Cambridge. All I mean is that I shouldn't have thought it was in the general run of your pursuits to listen to Berg or even Mozart when you should be fagging in Rec.

BOWLER. No, sir.

MASTER. But I'm not suggesting you give him up or anything so extreme. Just that you should reflect that too much too intense friendship can lead to too many complications for a chap who wants an uncluttered life. (*Pause.*) What do you say to that? (*Pause,* hold *on his face then cut to:*)

43. Interior Nindy's bedroom. *Straight in on* ALISON's *face.*

ALISON. That I've got a perfect right to be pregnant.

CHARLES (*who is scrabbling around in a drawer*). Of course you have.

ALISON (*puts* NINDY *down on the pot*). She patronises me.

CHARLES. I don't think she means to.

ALISON. Because she can't help it? Or because I make it un-avoidable?

CHARLES. I can't find any with special caps on.

ALISON. There's a blue tin. (*To* NINDY.) How are you doing, darling? That boy of theirs is a sly little brute.

CHARLES. Really? In what way?

ALISON. He's a mixer. He likes to stir things up - quite unnatural sophistication - piggy little eyes -

CHARLES. Darling, he's only six.

ALISON (*after a pause*). If he doesn't look out, he's going to have a heart attack.

CHARLES. At six?

ALISON. You know perfectly well. He boozed all through the day.

NINDY *on pot, sound of her peeing.*

ALISON. Oh clever girl! Look, Daddy, a wee-wee for you. (*She claps.*)

CHARLES *claps.*
ALISON *lifts* NINDY *off the pot, holds out her hand for the tin with the blue top, which she receives from* CHARLES, *spreads* NINDY *on the bed.*

ALISON. Can you honestly say that you still have anything in common?

Cut as if to: CHARLES's *face, but* come in, *instead,* on:

44. Interior. Master's study. *On* BOY's *face. He is sitting, as* BOWLER *was.*

BOY. Sir.

MASTER. Unless, that is, you've undertaken to supplement his education with some courses of your own.

BOY (*after a pause*). Sir?

MASTER. Those subjects, that is, in which you have a natural advantage.

BOY *says nothing.*

Is that what you're doing? (*Smiling.*)

BOY. We like talking about the same things, that's all.

MASTER. Really? Cricket, squash, athletics - you have an interest?

BOY. I like watching.

MASTER. But only when he's playing. No doubt. (*Smiles.*) he listens to you on Baudelaire because it's you he's interested in, not Baudelaire. What do you think this is all about?

BOY. I don't know, sir.

MASTER. Well, I'm asking you to be careful, that's all.

BOY. Sir. (*Little pause.*) What of, sir?

MASTER. Of yourself, and of your feelings. It's hard for you, I know, in that your health excludes you from a great deal of companionship, although I suspect you don't much regret that. You're very highly thought of, you know, by most of us - even if we find you a little frightening. I for one wouldn't dream of dictating the proper lines for friendship, there aren't any. But do remember, won't you, that your capacity for affection (*Hesitates.*) deserves various, mm, expressions. (*Pause.*) I'm not saying anything at all, it's sheer nonsense. (*Pause.*) You must find your own way. Nobody wishes you any harm. Please believe that. Do you?

See MASTER *from* BOY's *point of view. Cut as if to* BOY, *and in fact go to:*

45. Interior. Peter's study. *He is lighting a cigarette. A suggestion of desperation, props his hand under his chin, sits smoking.*

46. Interior. Charles's study. *He is sitting, staring ahead. A suggestion of despair.*

47. Interior. School Chapel. BOWLER's *face, as over the service (prayer). And cut to* BOY's *face, his eyes moving purposefully, as if looking for* BOWLER. *And cut to:*

48. Interior. Peter's study. Come in *on him coughing slightly, the cough goes on and on, gets out of control. He stubs out his cigarette fiercely, sits shaken.*

PETER. Christ!

PETER *gets up, hands not visible but sound of his pouring from a bottle to a glass. He sits down, coughs once or twice to clear his throat, then sits staring ahead.*

49. Interior. Music room. *Light on.* BOY *is staring out of window.*

50. Exterior. Music room window, *from* BOWLER's *point of view.* BOY's *face visible but indistinct.* Cut to BOWLER's *face, undecided, and* cut to:

51. Interior. *Very brief.* CHARLES *staring ahead.*

52. Interior. *Very brief.* PETER *staring ahead. This in fact from* HILARY's *point of view although not yet established.*

HILARY (*over*). Will you be long?

PETER (*turns*). No, I won't be long.

HILARY. Jeremy's sound asleep. He's exhausted, poor child. Not a peep out of him.

PETER. Well, I won't be long.

HILARY. Thank you. What's it like?

PETER. It's bloody hand-written, that's what it's like.

HILARY (*takes in the ash-tray, which has a number of butts in it. Then the glass*). Another drink? (*Pause.*) You're smoking too much.

PETER. Ah, that explains it.

HILARY. What?

PETER. Why I've got two hundred and fifty pages of hand-written novel to get through.

HILARY. Well, not tonight, I hope.

PETER. Some of it tonight.

HILARY. Why, if you're tired?

PETER *sighs.* HILARY *looks at him, turns, goes out.* PETER *stares at the empty door a moment, lights another cigarette.*

HILARY (*reappears at the door*). Look, I didn't ask to spend the day with your old school friend and his dull wife, and I didn't fill you full of wine all day to help you get through it, and I'm not pouring scotch down your throat to help you get over it. I don't know what's the matter with you, but I've had enough of everything today, including you.

PETER (*with insulting courtesy*). Have you?

> HILARY *glares at him, slams the door.*
> HILARY (*off*) *calls out something.*

PETER (*sits still for a moment, then bellows*). What?

HILARY (*re-opens the door, glares at him*). Would you kindly remember that Jeremy is asleep.

53. Interior. Charles's study. In on *his face, briefly. Move back, to* take in ALISON, *in her night-gown, holding two mugs.*

ALISON. But you are, I can tell.

CHARLES. No, contemplative.

ALISON. Then what are you contemplating?

CHARLES. I'm not sure. I don't think I'd fixed on a subject.

ALISON (*looks at him, troubled*). I wasn't trying to get at him, you know? (*Pause.*) Yes, I was.

CHARLES. I've never minded your not liking him.

ALISON. You mustn't. As long as you go on liking him -

CHARLES. Oh, I don't know. Old friends are like old habits. There comes a point when it doesn't matter any more whether you like them, they're what you've got.

ALISON. Is the same true of families?

CHARLES. Well, I don't keep adding to my circle of friends. But with my family, on the other hand - (*Smiles.*)

ALISON (*over*). I love you.

> Stay on CHARLES's *face, smiling and* cut to:

54. Interior. The music room. BOY *bent over the gramophone.
Then withdraw to* take in BOWLER, *hands in pockets, turned
away.*

BOWLER. I can only stay for a little bit. (*Formally.*)

BOY. I can't stay long either. (*Formally.*)

   Cut to:

55. Interior. Peter's bedroom. HILARY *lying asleep. On her face,
then* PETER *bends into* camera, *kisses her on the forehead, his
face withdraws.* HILARY's *eyes open slightly, slight smile.*

56. Interior. Charles's bedroom. On *his face, then* cut to:

   ALISON, *head on pillow, looking troubled,* CHARLES *puts
   out his hand, touches a lock of her hair, then moves* out of
   camera. ALISON *smiles. It is an unhappy smile.*
   Over, *Mozart and* fade into:

57. Interior. Music room. *As Mozart continues from previous
scene,* BOY *and* BOWLER *sitting, listening.* And over this:
Credits.

To Alan
for Ben, Simon, Peter and Charles

PLAINTIFFS AND DEFENDANTS

PLAINTIFFS AND DEFENDANTS was first presented by BBC Television on 16th October 1975 with the following cast:

PETER	Alan Bates
HILARY	Rosemary McHale
CHARLES	Dinsdale Landen
JEREMY	Daniel St. George
JOANNA	Georgina Hale
SALLUST	Simon Cadell
JOSH	Benjamin Whitrow
MRS SAWSBURY	Rosemary Martin
MR ROSE	Victor Langley
MAN 1	David Rose
DOCTOR	Tom Kempinski

Designed by Richard Henry
Directed by Michael Lindsay-Hogg
Produced by Kenith Trodd

1. Interior. Joanna's bed-sitter. PETER *is lying in bed, staring blankly into* camera.

JOANNA (*voice over*). . . . the thing about Josh, you see - well, he didn't discover about himself until he was nearly 30, it must have been awful for him.

PETER (*politely*). Must have been.

JOANNA (*voice over*). He's still the only person in the world I can talk to. Except you. I can talk to you, right?

PETER. Right.

JOANNA. You and Josh. You're incredibly different, though. He's a great talker and you're a great listener.

Cut to: JOANNA, *sitting in the corner of the bed, one shoulder hunched, smoking.*

JOANNA (*after a pause*). I'm being boring, aren't I, sorry. (*Sounds of* PETER *moving.*) Is it time, then?

PETER (*beginning to get dressed*). Well - nearly, I'm afraid, Jo.

JOANNA (*sits watching him*). It's funny how I always want to say something and then stop myself, all except this time. I'm sorry.

PETER (*dressing*). Say what?

JOANNA. Something to stop you going.

PETER. What have you said?

JOANNA. Nothing.

PETER. Oh, I see.

JOANNA. Do you want to go, is that it?

PETER. Of course not.

JOANNA. We've never spent a night together. Never.

PETER. No. I'm very bad tempered in the morning.

JOANNA. Are you?

PETER. Yes.

JOANNA. I can't imagine you bad tempered. Or anything but polite. No other moods except polite and randy. You are still randy for me, aren't you?

PETER *laughs, slightly embarrassed.*
JOANNA *laughs.*

JOANNA. You're the only man I've ever wanted, in this way. Ever.

PETER. What are you going to do this evening?

JOANNA. Oh, see Josh, I don't know. Do something to keep my mind off.

PETER. But that cover you're designing -

JOANNA. I'll start on that after midnight. I like to work after midnight.

PETER (*straightening from doing up his shoes*). You don't think that being free-lance cuts you off a bit. I know working in an office has its hazards but -

JOANNA. I wouldn't get much of a lunch-time, though, would I? And I need long lunch-hours, right? (*Smiling.*) When you have them?

PETER *smiles.*

I like them better even than evenings like this. The afternoons afterwards are like dreams, but the nights go on a bit. Go on then, make a run for it before I begin -

PETER *comes over, bends to kiss her.*
JOANN's *arms go around his neck, clasp him. Cut to:*
PETER's *face, in* JOANNA's *clasp, slightly desperate.*

JOANNA. No claims right?

PETER. I'll see you soon.

JOANNA (*letting him go*). Do you know when exactly?

PETER. Not exactly.

JOANNA. But soon?

PETER. Of course. It's going to be a hell of a week or two -

JOANNA *smiles, pained. Nods.*
PETER *raises his hand in salute, goes to the door, opens it.*
All this from JOANNA's *point of view.*
PETER *closes the door. When it's almost closed, see* JOANNA
from his point of view. She is sitting hunched, lighting another
cigarette. She turns her face, looks towards him. The door
obliterates her as it closes, and on the closed door, titles begin.

2. Exterior. Turkish baths. Titles continue. PETER *enters.*

3. Interior. Turkish baths. Titles. PETER *washing himself*
vigorously.

4. Exterior. Turkish baths. PETER *emerging, and*

5. Interior. Hall. Peter's house. *He enters, puts down brief-case,*
touches his hair, glances at watch. Then goes down hall, opens
door to kitchen. Cut to:

6. Hilary, *in her late thirties, is bent over a pile of papers marking*
them. Her brief-case is on the kitchen table. She looks up,
smiles.

HILARY. Hello.

PETER. Hi. (*Smiles back.*)

HILARY. Won't be a minute. (*Goes on marking.*)

PETER *picks up a mug from a kitchen shelf, sits down at the*
table with it, pours himself some coffee.

HILARY. You eaten?

PETER. Yes, I had a bite.

HILARY. Good. (*Scribbles something on the bottom of the*
essay.) You know that staff meeting last week - where I made

a few brief points about marking adults as if they were children, and the resistance from almost everyone?

PETER. But you carried the meeting.

HILARY. Until this evening. When a deputation of students demanded to know why we'd stopped grading their essays - they said it wasn't fair, as it meant they didn't know where they stood.

PETER. God!

HILARY. Well, this one knows where *she* stands all right. (*Pushing the essay away.*) C? plus.

PETER. She'll want to know more about that question-mark.

HILARY. How did the case go?

PETER (*thinks*). Oh, we lost. And the lecture?

HILARY. All right after ten minutes. I slid from *Little Dorrit* to *Bleak House* and got pretty knowing about the law. You look very dapper.

PETER. Do I?

HILARY. Oh, of course the party - how was it?

PETER. I didn't go.

HILARY. Why not?

PETER. Didn't feel in the mood.

HILARY (*has got up, comes around behind him, puts her hands on his shoulders, kisses him*). Your hair's wet.

PETER. Is it? (*Feels it.*) I had a shower.

HILARY. A *shower*, where?

PETER. I had a game of squash with Sallust. My pupil. It seemed a better idea than the party.

HILARY. And who won?

PETER. He did. Quite convincingly, actually.

HILARY. Darling, do you think you *ought* to play with him? He must be much younger than you and in top-notch condition - ?

PETER. Oh, I gave him a run, you know. (*Yawns.*)

HILARY. How's he getting on?

PETER. Oh, all right - gets on my tits now and then - passes me notes on points that help the Judges while away another 15 minutes of my life - ambitious little sod - he's all right.

Door opens. JEREMY *enters, he is about sixteen.*

Hello.

JEREMY. Hi. Is there an apple?

HILARY. In the bowl on top of the fridge.

JEREMY goes over, takes an apple.

PETER. Did you go to the flicks?

JEREMY. What?

PETER. Cinema? (*Little pause.*) Moving pictures. Movies. You said at breakfast you were going to the movies.

JEREMY. Oh. Yeah. (*Bites into his apple.*)

PETER. What did you see?

JEREMY. Oh, that famous Renoir thing.

HILARY. *La Grande Illusion*?

JEREMY thinks, shakes his head.

PETER. *La Règle du Jeu.*

JEREMY. Yeah.

PETER. I wish I'd known it was on, I could have just done with that this evening. That marvellous little Jewish Count - the rabbit shoot - every time I think of his face it makes me want to cry.

JEREMY. What, the rabbit's?

HILARY. Didn't you like it, darling?

JEREMY. Yeah, I did. Quite.

PETER. Oh come on, Jeremy!

HILARY. Darling, if he didn't like it, he didn't like it. They've got to discover their own classics -

PETER. Well, what are they?

HILARY. Darling, what's your idea of a classic?

JEREMY. Classic? (*Thinks.*) I never think about whether it's a *classic* or not. Just about whether I liked it.

PETER. And you didn't like *Règle du Jeu*?

JEREMY (*who has been moving towards the door*). I said I quite liked it.

HILARY. That's true, darling. He did say he quite liked it.

JEREMY *goes out.*

PETER (*after a pause*). He didn't like it.

HILARY. Perhaps he tried, though.

PETER. Is that what the question-mark's for? In C question-mark plus.

HILARY. You didn't give him much chance.

PETER. A chance? With Renoir? He claims to be what they call a film buff, which I thought might mean that he could end up editing or directing or even reviewing the bloody things but he talks as if he already distributes them.

Cut to:

7. Interior. The bedroom. HILARY *in bed, reading, spectacles on, seen from* PETER's *point of view, as he hangs his trousers on the chair. She looks up.*

HILARY. I don't remember getting you yellow knickers.

PETER. No, I picked up a fresh pair, for the game, I'd forgotten - (*Coughs.*)

HILARY. That cough. You've got to stop. (*Goes back to her book.*)

PETER *climbs into bed, lies staring ahead, and* cut to:
A blown-up picture of a Junior Colts cricket eleven, seen from PETER's *point of view. First, the picture as a whole, then various faces, ending with possibly the young* PETER's. *Cut back to his face, smiling slightly, then frowns as a very light snoring noise impinges. He turns, looks down at* HILARY, *who has fallen asleep.*
PETER *gently takes the book from her hands, puts it on her side of the bed, then the spectacles, lays them on top of the book, looks down at her face,* cut to:
HILARY's *face, in sleep.*
PETER *kisses her forehead, and* cut to:

8. Interior. Peter's room in chambers. SALLUST *sitting in a corner.* PETER *gesturing a woman in her middle thirties into a seat. With her,* ROSE, *a middle-aged solicitor, who also sits down.*

MRS SAWSBURY (*after a pause*). I didn't realise there'd be two of you -

PETER. Mr Sallust is my pupil. It's customary for him to sit in, I hope you don't mind. He'll be helping me with your case. Mr Rose, I've had a look at the statement Mrs Sawsbury gave you - there are just a few things I'd like to clear up. Did you explain to Mrs Sawsbury?

ROSE. She knows you're to be her Counsel.

PETER. Good. Mrs Sawsbury, I'll have to ask you some fairly brutal questions, but they're questions the other side are bound to put to you, so we must be quite clear on your responses, all right?

MRS SAWSBURY. Yes.

PETER. Now - (*Looking at the statement.*) now your present income comes entirely from the alimony settled on you by your husband, that's right, isn't it?

ROSE. Yes.

MRS SAWSBURY. No, I've got a job now.

PETER (*glances at* ROSE *very briefly, then away again*). What job?

MRS SAWSBURY. Usherette, in a cinema.

PETER. West End cinema?

MRS SAWSBURY. Yes.

PETER. And what does that bring you?

MRS SAWSBURY. Twenty pounds a week.

ROSE. You didn't mention this to me, Mrs Sawsbury.

MRS SAWSBURY. I only started last week. But I've been looking for work for a long time - we can't live on the alimony, not these days.

PETER. No, of course not. And you haven't asked for more from your ex-husband?

MRS SAWSBURY. No, I never wanted his money anyway, I'd rather do without his help. I thought (*Looks at* ROSE.) it would make a difference if I could bring them up without his help.

PETER. What hours do you work?

MRS SAWSBURY. Three afternoons and three evenings.

PETER. Sounds rather nice. And who looks after the children?

MRS SAWSBURY. I've got them into one of the Council nursery schools.

PETER. But your oldest child - the boy - Kevin - is old enough to go to school, isn't he?

MRS SAWSBURY. I've got the choice until next year. They can stay at the nursery until half-past-five.

PETER. Oh yes. Very practical. (*Little pause.*) And in the evening? On the three evenings ? -

MRS SAWSBURY. I have a friend who looks after them.

PETER. Gives them their tea and puts them to bed?

MRS SAWSBURY. And stays in with them.

PETER. You don't pay your friend?

MRS SAWSBURY. No, I don't.

PETER. A real friend, then. (*Smiles, little pause.*) Now what do *you* estimate your husband's income at?

MRS SAWSBURY. Well, it varies - I know it's got more since he left - but it goes from year to year.

ROSE. In his statement he puts it between four and five thousand a year. Three and a half would be more accurate.

MRS SAWSBURY. Anyway, I don't see what that's got to do with it, besides he's got another child now. That's what's so unfair.

PETER. It's part of their case that he can give your children certain advantages, you see.

MRS SAWSBURY. He can't give them my love.

PETER. What about your ex-husband's new wife?

MRS SAWSBURY. They don't *know* her - except as somebody

who stuffs them with chocolates and takes them to the pictures. And their coloured TV, of course, but they're not advantages, are they?

PETER (*smiles*). Only if you like Westerns.

MRS SAWSBURY. Lucille hates them.

PETER. But you'd agree that they get on reasonably well with her? Your children do - ?

MRS SAWSBURY. They don't mind going.

PETER. Do they look forward to it?

MRS SAWSBURY. Only for the treats. But they wouldn't miss them if they weren't promised by their father.

PETER (*looks quickly at* ROSE, *who acknowledges the look, then down at the statement*). Mrs Sawsbury, I said some of my questions would be brutal. Well, here's one. Are you ready?

MRS SAWSBURY *nods.*

Are you living with anyone?

MRS SAWSBURY. It's my flat, I've the lease.

PETER. Well then, is anybody living with you?

MRS SAWSBURY. No.

PETER. It's very important, Mrs Sawsbury. The other side claims that there is a man - they have evidence -

MRS SAWSBURY. No.

PETER. The friend who looks after the children. Is it a man or a woman?

MRS SAWSBURY (*after a pause*). A man.

PETER. And does he ever spend the night in your flat?

The telephone rings.

Sorry. (*Picks it up quickly.*) Hello. (*Little pause.*) Look, I'm sorry, but I can't talk, I'm in the middle of a conference. (*Little pause.*) I can't say at the moment. Sorry. Goodbye. (*Puts the telephone down.*) Sorry. (*Looks momentarily distracted.*) Um, yes, does he, Mrs Sawsbury?

MRS SAWSBURY. Well only sometimes, when he's late back.

PETER. And does he spend those nights in your bed? I'm sorry, Mrs Sawsbury.

MRS SAWSBURY (*after a pause*). Yes.

PETER. And do you have any plans to marry?

MRS SAWSBURY. He's a Catholic, and so's his wife. (*Pause.*) Well, why not, we're both lonely, his wife hates him, she doesn't mind, his daughter's grown-up, *she's* married now, nobody cares - and *he's* got somebody in *his* bed, hasn't he, and if he can do it, why shouldn't I?

PETER. I'm not judging you, Mrs Sawsbury, but I must know, for your sake, what we're to expect in court.

MRS SAWSBURY. Well, what *am* I to expect? I mean, he can't just come after two years without doing anything except send his cheques in, and take my children away because he's got more money than me because he can work and I can't and because he's married again. He can't do that - that's not justice, is it?

PETER. Why do *you* think he wants them back?

MRS SAWSBURY. To spite me.

PETER. He says he loves them.

MRS SAWSBURY. Then why did he leave them in the first place. If you love people you stay for them, don't you? I didn't take them away from him, he took himself away because he said he couldn't stand it any more, and now he's trying to take them away. Everything's always come so easily to him, but they're not going to. I won't let them. (*Pause.*) I won't, you know.

Cut to:

9. Interior. Peter's room in chambers. MRS SAWSBURY *and* ROSE *gone.* PETER *sitting back, smoking,* SALLUST *watching him.*

PETER. Well, Tommy, what do you think?

SALLUST. She's very unengaging.

PETER. Well, not to her elderly Catholic lover. Nor, perhaps, to her children. So possibly not to the judge - at least, if he's elderly, Catholic and childish. Some of them are.

SALLUST. I hope she doesn't get on to her ex-husband when she gives evidence. It'll seem as if she's only hanging on to them to spite him.

PETER. He's a swine. No, he probably isn't.

The telephone rings.

PETER (*hesitates, fractionally, picks it up*). Yes. Oh, well put her through, please, I'm free now. (*Listens.*) Yes, yes, that'll be all right. Goodbye. (*Puts the telephone down.*)

10. Interior. Joanna's bed-sitter. PETER *and* JOANNA *are standing in the middle of the room.*

JOANNA. I've got a lot of ham and assorted crudities.

PETER. I'm not hungry, thanks.

JOANNA. There's some scotch.

PETER. God no. I've got some briefs to look at this afternoon. Well, how are you, then? Been, um, doing anything interesting?

JOANNA. Oh, a few covers from those people where we met.

PETER. Good.

JOANNA. A few ups and downs with Josh, right?

PETER. Josh?

JOANNA. That friend of mine I told you about. His affair with that actor came to a sticky end, I'm sure I told you. (*Pause.*) Anyway, he's been in one of his depressions, losing hair and fattening, so I've been on call as his favourite mother. It's too ridiculous.

PETER. Poor Jo. (*Little pause.*) Poor Josh, come to think of it.

JOANNA *laughs and* cut to: PETER *suppressing wince.*

JOANNA. Sorry about phoning. But your coming around at lunch-time was such a habit and then you stopped - I worried whether you were all right, right?

PETER. No, I'm sorry I had to be so circumspect, there was somebody with me. (*Pause.*) Sorry, by the way, I haven't been able to get around, it's been very difficult, what with one case and another . . . haven't had a moment . . . how'd you get hold of my work number, by the way?

JOANNA. I looked it up.

PETER. That was very clever of you.

JOANNA (*laughs*). Matter of fact, I did manage to get a glimpse of you.

PETER. Where?

JOANNA. On the tube, actually. I was in the next carriage and saw you through the windows, it was weird.

PETER. Weird, really, what was I doing?

JOANNA. Well, do you really want to know? (*Laughs.*) Well, you were smoking and you had some work in your lap, and you were looking at a girl who was sitting a bit down from you. She was very young and she was reading an enormous book. I made one of those calculations only unlib. spinsters are supposed to make, you know, that she could just about have been your daughter.

PETER (*lighting a cigarette*). How long did you watch me for?

JOANNA. Oh, a few stops. Any of your cases been interesting?

PETER. Only if you're interested in mess. And defeat.

JOANNA. Well, one side usually wins, you told me, right?

PETER. At the moment, I appear to be representing the other side. Why didn't you join me at one of the stops?

JOANNA. I wasn't sure you wanted to see me. To tell you the truth I was following you.

PETER (*after a pause*). Really? How far?

JOANNA. Well, to your front door. And then Jeremy came up on his mo-ped - it was Jeremy, right? He went in.

PETER. On a mo-ped and through the front door, yes, that was probably my son.

JOANNA (*laughs. There is a pause*). I shouldn't have told you, right? I swore to God I wouldn't.

PETER. It doesn't matter.

JOANNA. It matters to me, as I'm trying to cut down on humiliations.

PETER. That's because you know you're (*Hesitates.*) worth more than a lunch-time doss-down with a married man.

JOANNA. That's all it's been, then?

PETER. Well, it's not been much else for you, I shouldn't think. Jo, I'm sorry, it was all my fault, I know that.

JOANNA (*smiles in pain*). Well, I thought *you'd* give me my cards with some style. I mean, be original . . .

PETER. I'm sorry.

JOANNA. For the past two weeks, since you stopped coming, I've been waiting by the phone. I didn't dare go out, even if it meant missing a chance of a commission. I even thought you might be ill. (*Laughs.*) I worried for you, or an accident or (*Shrugs.*) - is it because of following you?

PETER. You did know I was married, I told you at once. I have a life - (*Pause.*) - also I meant it when I said you were worth more - I mean - (*Smiles.*) - there are lots of males between homos like Josh and husbands like me, it's sad that you should waste yourself -

JOANNA. Couldn't you say outright that you've stopped fancying me and I've become a nuisance?

PETER. I've stopped fancying you and you've become a nuisance.

There is a pause, JOANNA *shocked.*

Is that really any better? It's certainly not true. I still fancy . . .

JOANNA (*cutting in*). Yes, well, you can go now, if you want.

PETER (*makes to say something, checks himself, goes to the door*). I'm sorry about the clichés. My manners have been appalling, right the way through.

JOANNA *stares blankly, smoking,* Hold *on her, then* cut to:
PETER *beginning to close the door behind him.*
JOANNA *lets out a wail, it turns into a scream, she gets up, races crazily around the room, wailing, knocking over work-table etc.* Cut to: PETER's *face appalled, caught at the door and on this* cut to:

11. Exterior. London suburban garden. Point of view *upstairs window.*

ALISON, *very pregnant,* HILARY *and five children ranging from three to twelve. Their cries muffled.* Cut to:

12. Charles's face *staring out of the window.*

PETER (*voice over*). If I hadn't gone back I'd have spent the next three months waiting to hear of her suicide - or worse.

CHARLES (*waving, smiling down*). Would she really go that far?

PETER cut to *him, on a polystyrene bag, in an ascetic male preserve, do-it-yourself book-cases, school text-books, unmarked and marked school essays on the desk. Around the walls there are pictures of school groups. One of these is the same as the one in* PETER's *and* HILARY's *bedroom.*

PETER. The point is, one doesn't know. At least, I don't. But once I *had* gone back in, it was bound to move in a fairly predictable sequence, a slap on the chops to stop her hysterics, a cup of tea to soothe her, a cuddle to stop her trembling, a fuck to - (*Gestures.*)

CHARLES (*sits in the opposite polystyrene*). Do you think that's ended it?

PETER. I don't know. There's no way of glossing a fuck, is there? I tried to make it forlorn and farewell.

CHARLES. Couldn't you have said something?

PETER. What? If I said anything ambiguous, she would have ignored the other and real meaning. If anything explicit -

CHARLES. You'd have been picking up the furniture again. I thought you'd decided to give up that sort of thing anyway.

PETER. This sort of thing I never tried to take up.

CHARLES. Well, casual affairs.

PETER. Yes. Although there's nothing casual about this one now. Yes, I had given it up. But there was a party and I - I had some fantasy that I might be lucky with some pertly little creature - dreams, dreams. Because there was old reality standing by herself in a corner and myself gravitating ineluctably towards her as usual. I can't explain it. (*Little pause.*) She's ghastly! Look, old cheese, you did mutter something about a -

CHARLES (*gets up, goes to scotch, syphon and two glasses on the desk*). But in bed, surely?

PETER. Yes, but so ravenous. Making love to somebody you can't stand but who's infatuated with you makes you believe you have a soul. Otherwise why do you feel so rotten? And afterwards the mandatory post-coital cigarette, she smokes with a shoulder hunched (*Imitates* JOANNA *smoking.*) and if I attempt a joke, her *laugh.* (*Imitates* JOANNA *laughing.*)

CHARLES *laughs.* PETER *laughs slightly, offers* CHARLES *a cigarette.* CHARLES *with a slight smile shakes his head.*

PETER. And then the endless squalid complications of turning up at home smelling just right - not freshly showered but not, of course - oh God! (*Sits depressed for a moment.*) You've given up smoking.

CHARLES. Apparently I'm lucky in my metabolism. I scarcely suffered. I had to take over the soccer one afternoon, and I couldn't keep up with the under-14s. And I suppose I believe school-teachers ought to set an example - and as a father, come to that.

PETER. I set just the right example for Jeremy. He models himself on everything I'm not. My vices have moulded an ascetic - have you given up alcohol too?

CHARLES. Well - yes, really.

PETER. Christ, Charlie!

CHARLES. You don't think - (*Going to the window, looking down.*) Cut to:

13. Exterior. *From* CHARLES's point of view. Alison *and* HILARY *talking, children playing.*

CHARLES (*voice over*). You don't think you should tell Hilary?

PETER (*voice over*). Good God, why?

Cut to:

14. Interior. Charles.

CHARLES. Well, if this girl's as unstable as you say, she might

- you know. And it would be better if it came from you first.

PETER. I'd rather take the risk. She's finding her new lecture-ship exhausting enough - I don't want to create any unneces-sary - (*Gestures.*)

CHARLES. Yes, but if the girl does - it would be much worse. Besides, she'd understand, surely?

PETER. Understand what? That I'd been unfaithful to her for ten years, on and off. You don't think she'd settle for one infidelity, do you - we'd be working back through our married life together - (*Shudders.*) The habits of confession and recrimination root very quickly, you know. I hear enough of them at work, I don't want to go through them at home. (*Gets up, goes to the window, looks out.*) When's it due?

CHARLES. Next week some time.

PETER. Alison looks amazingly sprightly.

CHARLES. Oh, she scarcely notices any more. Except when she's not.

PETER. Will this be your last?

CHARLES. Only if it's a boy. She'll go on until she produces one -

15. Exterior. Garden. *From* PETER's *point of view.* ALISON, HILARY *and the children. Joined by a nubile girl of about 15.*

PETER (*voice over*). How old *is* Caroline?

CHARLES (*voice over*). Fifteen.

PETER (*voice over, keeping* CAROLINE *in perspective as she bends over one of the other children*). Mm.

CHARLES (*voice over*). Something I better warn you about, Pete.

16. Interior The study. PETER *turns, faces* CHARLES.

CHARLES. We've gone vegetarian, I'm afraid.

Cut to:

1⁷. Interior. Peter's and Hilary's kitchen. PETER *is washing up a few dishes. He is in his pyjamas.* JEREMY *enters, goes to fridge, takes out a bottle of milk, pours some into a glass.*

PETER. Is that all you want?

JEREMY. Yeah.

PETER. Have a good day?

JEREMY. It was all right.

PETER. Get a lot done?

JEREMY. Mmm?

PETER. Work. You were going to spend the day on your work, weren't you? Your 'A' levels?

JEREMY. I've just come in.

PETER. I know you've just come in. But before you went out –

JEREMY. I did some.

PETER (*after a pause*). Good.

JEREMY (*goes towards the kitchen door, stops*). The telephone kept going.

PETER. Oh. Who was it?

JEREMY. I don't know. When I answered they hung up. From a call-box.

PETER. Probably for you then?

JEREMY. No.

PETER. How do you know?

JEREMY. Because they wouldn't have hung up when I answered.

PETER. But the call-boxes these days – (*Turning away.*) The vandals have scarcely left one intact. (*Turns back.*) Tell me –

JEREMY *is exiting from the kitchen.* PETER *turns back to the sink. Above, the sound of the telephone ringing.* Cut to:

18. Interior. The bedroom. HILARY *is lying in bed, spectacles on, reading. One hand extended casually over the telephone. Sound of a cough, door opening, closing.*

HILARY. God, that cough of yours.

PETER. Wasn't that the phone?

HILARY. Yes.

The telephone rings.

HILARY (*picks it up, gaze still on the book, waits*). 348 0720. Hello. (*Puts the telephone down.*)

PETER. Who is it?

HILARY. Don't know. The pips are doing their endless pipping -

PETER. Probably somebody for Jeremy.

HILARY. Shouldn't think so.

PETER. Why not? (*Getting undressed.*)

HILARY. He's very considerate.

PETER (*looks at her in astonishment*). Even if he were, he'd hardly be phoning us up, as he's already in the house. One of his friends -

HILARY. Not at this hour.

PETER *gets into bed, lies back, looks across at the Junior Colts picture.*

I wish Jeremy had come today. Caroline's really very nice -

PETER. A little young, surely.

HILARY. What did you and Charlie talk about upstairs, or were you just hiding?

PETER. Oh, about all the things he's given up. Which is really the last 20 years, when you think about it. What did you and Alison talk about?

HILARY. Her womb. She was admiring it for its fertility - rather as one admires Dickens for his.

PETER (*laughs*). Macrobiotic. Onion and parsnip stew, Russian salad, fruit salad, no nicotine, no alcohol, Christ! (*Coughs slightly.*)

HILARY. It's economics, of course. They can't have children *and* all the other vices. They do look extremely healthy on it, though. (*Pause.*) Well, they're our best friends. You and Charlie had a grubby public school dorm affair when you

were passing through adolescence together, and you did your
national service at the same barracks. So now they're our
best friends at 38.

PETER. I neither had a dorm affair nor did my national service
with Alison.

HILARY. And I suppose they'll be best friends to the end, won't
they? They'll go on and on, Sunday lunches and monthly
dinners until something happens to change them, a death
possibly. (*Shudders.*) Why did I say that? (*Laughs.*) Anyway,
I suppose we love them, don't we?

PETER. I don't know. Old friends are like old habits. Once
you've got them it's too late to wonder whether you actually
want them. (*Coughs.*)

HILARY. If Charles can do something about his smoking, can't
you?

PETER. Mmmm.

HILARY (*turns her head, looks at him*). Don't you care that I
care?

PETER *turns his head, looks at her, puts his hand out, touches
her on the cheek, then suddenly leans over, kisses her.*

HILARY. Please make an effort.

PETER *kisses her more passionately, then more passionately
again.*

HILARY (*pushes him away*). That's not the issue. Besides, I've
got a hard day tomorrow. I'm giving a lunch-time lecture as
well as the evening seminars. And a Board of Studies meeting -

PETER *looks at her, falls back on the pillow.*

HILARY. Oh, don't take offence. (*Pause.*) All right, do. (*Turns
out her light, turns her back on* PETER.)

PETER — *his light still on, lies staring across the room, and
cut to: The photograph of the Junior Colts. See it in close up,
then moving from face to face, pausing on a face that could
be Peter's.*

HILARY (*voice over*). Look, it's not bloody fair, I must get some
sleep if I'm to cope tomorrow!

PETER *blinks, turns.* HILARY *is sitting up in bed, glaring at
him:*

Please turn out your light! (*Leans across him, turns it out.*)

There is a silence. A very slight cough from PETER.

Give us a cuddle then.

Another silence, then the sound of PETER *getting out of bed.*

(*After a pause.*). Pete?

The sound of the door closing.

Silly bugger! (*To herself.*)

19. Interior. The kitchen. PETER *is sitting at the table, smoking.*

HILARY (*at the door*). Do you prefer this to sleeping with me?

PETER. It's more stimulating.

   HILARY *stares at him, then goes out, closing the door,*
   emphatically.
   PETER *sits for a moment, then stubs out his cigarette, gets up*
   hesitates, goes out.

20. Interior. The bedroom. HILARY *is in bed, her light on.*
PETER *gets in beside her, puts his light off.*

HILARY. Well, what *is* the matter with you?

PETER. Nothing.

HILARY. Then that's all right then, isn't it? (*Turns her light off.*)

   There is a pause. HILARY *turns her light on, looks down at*
   PETER, *lying with his hands folded under his head.*

You're being exceptionally childish.

PETER. What?

   HILARY *turns her light off.*

PETER (*turns his light on*). What do you mean - childish?

   HILARY *turns away from him.*

PETER. Christ! (*Turns his light off.*)

   There is a pause.
   HILARY *turns her light on. Looks at* PETER *again, gets out*

of bed. PETER *sits up, stares after her, as* HILARY *goes out of room.*

PETER. Oh Christ! (*Gets out of the bed, follows* HILARY *out, slamming the door behind him.*)

21. Interior. Kitchen. HILARY *and* PETER *sitting opposite each other, smoking.*

HILARY (*talking in a whisper*) - no use your blaming me, I'm upset by it too but I can't help it. But you know I'm not off you, and you know I love you, it's just that - it's a strain, at the moment, I keep revolving the next day's lectures or what's worse, last week's, I really wonder whether I should have undertaken them, I don't seem to have the stomach for addressing large groups on - and I keep wondering whether I'm boring them or stupefying them and what the difference is. (*Pause.*) Am I in danger then?

PETER (*also whispering*). What? What of?

HILARY. Of your looking elsewhere. I don't think I could bear that.

PETER. Don't be silly.

HILARY. I do worry about it, you know. And the unfairness of it.

PETER. It's not at all unfair. I *was* being childish -

HILARY. No, I meant the unfairness to me. Or us. Women. How when I'm in my forties, which is tomorrow almost, you'll still be very attractive -

PETER. So will you.

HILARY. And then when I'm in my fifties - or when you're in your sixties even, going by current trends - I'll just be a woman in my sixties as far as you're concerned -

PETER. You don't believe that.

HILARY. I'm talking about my worries, not my beliefs. I can perfectly well imagine myself struggling not to check your pockets or your underwear drawer before doing both probably - it's very humiliating. (*Pause.*) You know damn well I'm not frigid -

PETER (*emotionally*). Darling! (*Takes her hand.*) Look, let me tell you -

Door opens. JEREMY *enters. There is a pause.*

JEREMY. Anyone want a cup of tea?

HILARY. Darling, shouldn't you be in bed?

JEREMY. I've got a free class tomorrow. (*Putting the kettle on.*) Don't have to be in until ten. (*Sits down.*)

HILARY *and* PETER *exchange glances. There is a silence.*

HILARY. What have you been doing?

JEREMY. Oh nothing really.

Hold *on the three of them for a moment.*

PETER (*after a long pause*). So much for Pascal.

JEREMY. What?

PETER. Wasn't it Pascal who said that all human evil came from our not being able to sit alone in a room, doing nothing?

HILARY. If we *could* all do that, there wouldn't be any humans left to do it. (*Brightly.*)

Cut to:

22. Interior. Bedroom. *Lights out.*

HILARY (*voice over*). I know he does.

PETER. So do I. In that it would be most unnatural if he didn't. But that would only account for the odd half hour of his day, surely. What does he do for the rest of the time?

HILARY. Recuperates.

PETER *laughs, so does* HILARY *and* cut to:

23. Interior Peter's room in chambers. ROSE, MRS SAWSBURY, SALLUST *and* PETER. PETER *clearing his throat, waits.*

MRS SAWSBURY. But it was only the once. It only happened the once. He doesn't drink heavily as a rule, but he was feeling very low, his daughter's husband had been very rude to him, and he went to the pub. He's not a drinking man. I don't know where they got hold of this - this sort of lie.

PETER. The trouble is, it's not exactly a lie. He did hit them, unfortunately.

MRS SAWSBURY. Only the boy.

PETER. And pushed the girl.

MRS SAWSBURY. He didn't hurt them.

PETER. Probably not - as they made so much noise. They wouldn't if they had been really frightened.

MRS SAWSBURY. He's very fond of them, and they know it. He was ashamed afterwards, he cried.

There is a pause. The telephone rings on the desk.

PETER. Excuse me. Who? Look, I can't take any calls, I'm - what? Who? I haven't got an appointment - (*Listens.*) Well, he can try then. (*Puts the telephone down, slightly abstracted.*) Sorry.

There is a pause.

MRS SAWSBURY. It's not fair if something like that counts against us. Will it?

PETER (*pulling himself together*). One can never be quite sure what does count. We'll do our best to make the Judge understand.

24. Interior. Peter and Sallust.

PETER. They've got a private detective of course.

SALLUST. Shouldn't we get one?

PETER. It's too late. They'll be living their lives as if we already have.

SALLUST. Of all the times to get drunk and clout the kids! Do you think we've got a chance?

PETER. Of what?

SALLUST. Of winning.

PETER. Oh yes. So has opposing counsel. I shouldn't think anybody else has, though.

The telephone rings.

PETER (*answers it*). Still there? (*Looks at his watch.*) All right.
(*Puts the telephone down.*) Don't feel up to anybody else's
misery just at the moment.

Door opens.

Mr James, isn't it?

JOSH. Yes.

JOSH *enters. He is in his mid-thirties, with a strained, unhappy-
looking face.*

PETER. This is my pupil, Mr Sallust. You haven't come to us
through a solicitor, have you, Mr James?

JOSH. No.

PETER. I should warn you that really you should see a solicitor -

JOSH. It's a private matter you see. (*Pause.*) About a friend of
mine. Miss um, Pelley.

PETER (*puzzled for a second, then controlling himself*). Oh.
Then perhaps, Tommy - ?

SALLUST. Of course. (*Goes out.*)

There is a pause.

JOSH. I don't know if she's mentioned me to you - Josh.

PETER. Yes, I believe she did, once or twice. (*Lights a cigarette.*)

JOSH. I'm sorry to come in on you like this - I didn't know
what else to do.

PETER *waits.*

I'm frightened.

PETER. What of?

JOSH. Her. *For* her, that is. You see, I went around last night,
she wasn't normal. Well - even for her. She was talking rather
wildly -

PETER. What about?

JOSH. You. She hasn't stopped that, but there's a kind of
despair, you know, beyond her usual - desperation - (*Looks at*

PETER.) You see, you're the third man in a row to go wrong on her.

PETER. I see. (*His hand is trembling slightly.*) I was under the impression that you and she -

JOSH. Oh no. I'm homosexual. I slept with her once or twice, when she needed comforting. I expect she makes more out of it to other people - at the moment I'm no use to her. I would be if I could.

PETER. I don't know what I can do.

JOSH. If you could just bring yourself to talk to her - She wouldn't let me in this morning, but I could hear her through the door, whimpering - I know how awful this must be for you, I'm sorry to ask.

PETER *sits smoking, trying to control himself.*

I expect all you wanted was a quick lay. It's not fair, is it?

PETER (*smiles shakily*). Thank you.

Cut to:

25. Interior. Joanna's bed-sitter. JOANNA *is in bed, in pyjamas.* PETER *is sitting in the chair beside the bed.*

PETER. But surely you must see a doctor.

JOANNA (*smiling bravely*). No, it's only flu, I tell you. (*Laughs.*) You would come around suddenly after all this time and catch me in this state. (*Lights a cigarette.*)

PETER. Should you?

JOANNA. Won't hurt me. Anyway, the number *you* smoke - (*Affectionately.*)

PETER. Yes.

JOANNA. I couldn't actually make out from our last time whether you were going to come back.

PETER. Well, now you know. (*Smiling.*)

JOANNA. Yes. I feel better - you've got a medicinal smile.

PETER. That must mean it's hard to swallow.

JOANNA. What? (*Laughs.*)

PETER. Can I make you some tea - or -

JOANNA (*shakes her head*). You've been very busy then?

PETER. Yes.

JOANNA. I haven't followed you again.

PETER. What about phoning?

JOANNA (*looks at him*). Mm?

PETER. Have you tried phoning me?

JOANNA. I won't do it again. I just wanted to hear your voice . . .

PETER. Instead you heard my wife's and my son's.

> JOANNA *lies down, turns her face away, begins to cry.*
> PETER *looks at her with a kind of desperate irritation, then moves over to the bed, takes the cigarette away from her fingers, puts it into the ashtray.*

JOANNA (*puts one hand into his lap*). You want to go, don't you?

PETER. No - it's just that I've got to be back in chambers -

JOANNA. You can go now, if you like.

PETER. No, no, I can stay on a bit.

JOANNA (*cries out*). I love you.

> PETER *closes his eyes in horror.*

> I won't do anything to make you unhappy, I swear. If I can just see you -

> PETER *fumbles with his free hand for a cigarette.* Cut to:

26. Interior. Hilary's and Peter's bedroom. HILARY *is lying in bed, staring up at the ceiling. Her face is tight with anger. There is the sound of coughing,* PETER *enters, naked. He is carrying his clothes. He dumps shoes on the floor, goes to a drawer, chucks pants and socks on to the chair.*

HILARY. How's Jeremy?

PETER. He's in his room.

HILARY. But how is he?

PETER. I don't know. He's in his room and I'm here.

HILARY. I thought you might have looked in on him, to say good night.

PETER. I said it from my usual place, a tentative foot or two on the other side of his door.

HILARY. Yes, but I thought you might have looked in on him tonight.

PETER. Really? Why?

HILARY. To apologise.

PETER. For what?

HILARY. For being so offensive.

PETER. Offensive? I thought we were having a high-powered discussion as to the relative merits of Laurel and Hardy -

HILARY. *You* were having the discussion.

PETER. I allowed him to display the full range of his critical vocabulary. I counted five 'whats', and seven 'yeahs', and six 'all rights'.

HILARY. We know you did. You counted them out loud, if you remember. He merely said that he *quite enjoyed* Laurel and Hardy.

PETER. No, he didn't. He said they were all right. And that's all he said.

HILARY. Why should he say more - especially under an assault like that.

PETER. I've heard you talk about students in your seminars with *their* 'all rights', and 'quite liked its' -

HILARY. Jeremy is not a student in my seminar. He's our 16-year-old son. Whose behaviour, I might say, was remarkably adult under the circumstances.

PETER. And who provides the circumstances? Not every youth these days is lucky enough to have a father who conforms to the propaganda, crop-headed, authoritarian, grammatical -

HILARY. His sole offence this evening was to be younger and nicer than you.

PETER. That makes two offences, both serious. (*Gets into bed, coughs slightly.*) Anyway, *he* didn't seem to mind.

HILARY. If you really think that, then you're being stupid. (*Switches off her light.*)

PETER *lies staring angrily ahead.* Cut to:
Junior Colts picture.

HILARY. You've been ghastly all evening. The one evening I have off during the week and when Jeremy's home - all of us having a proper family dinner together, which I spent the afternoon thinking about and getting ready - and you come home scarcely able to look at anyone, you drank too much before the meal, and then ruined the meal with your ego-istical - it was unforgivable.

PETER. You think that unforgivable? You should come to court one day and find out the sort of thing *my* sort of people don't forgive each other.

HILARY. Would you like Jeremy - and myself - to be that sort of people?

PETER. At least I'd know where I was. A son who scarcely addresses a remark to me, a wife who moralises and black-mails -

HILARY *hits him. They sit glaring at each other, then* HILARY *collapses back on the bed.* PETER *remains sitting upright, staring at the Junior Colts picture.* Cut to *it, then* back to PETER, *as sound of muffled sobs over. He sits staring im-passively, then turns, looks down at* HILARY.
HILARY *is lying, her shoulders shaking.*
PETER *looks down at her, his expression quite detached, but sad. He leans over, then puts his arms around her, lifts her up against himself.*

PETER. I'm sorry. I didn't mean that.

HILARY *struggles against him, almost frantically.*

PETER (*clutches her to him*). Don't, don't, don't, don't. (*Soothingly.*)

HILARY *subsides. Occasional deep sobs.*

PETER. You know I love you. (*Strokes her hair. Coughs very slightly.*) You know that.

HILARY. And who else do you love?

PETER. Jeremy.

HILARY. And no one else? No girl or woman that -

PETER. No one else. Nothing else either. Perhaps that's my trouble.

HILARY. You used to love your work.

PETER. It's not very lovable at the moment.

> PETER *strokes her hair, then kisses her on the mouth. Kisses her again, more passionately. Begins to caress her.* HILARY *at first resists, then acquiesces, then begins to respond with passion.* Cut to:
> PETER *is lying back, coughing.*

HILARY (*leaning over him, concerned*). That was a race against time. Or death, it felt like. You certainly don't love yourself, do you?

> *The telephone rings.* HILARY *and* PETER *look at each other.*

HILARY. 348 0720. (*Listens.*) Pips. (*Looks at* PETER, *puts the telephone down thoughtfully.*)

PETER (*urgently*). Take it off the hook. (*Reaches across.*)

> *The telephone rings.*

HILARY (*picks it up*). 348 0720. (*Waits. Pause.*) Which hospital? (*Little pause.*) Yes, we'll take the call. Here - *you'd* better - (*Hands the telephone to* PETER.) It's a hospital - they've reversed charges.

PETER (*clutching the telephone, waits, then*). Hello - I can't hear - which hospital. (*Listens.*) Who?

> HILARY *watching intently.*

Yes, it is. (*Pause.*) Charlie, hello! What - oh Charlie, wonderful - it's Charlie - a son!

HILARY (*smiling*). Thank God!

> *Cut to:*

27. Interior. Joanna's bed-sitter. JOANNA, *fully dressed, is sitting in a corner of the bed, smoking.* PETER *is standing.*

JOANNA. I thought this was one of your late nights. When you're not expected home -

PETER. Yes, it is.

JOANNA. And so you've just looked in to say you could only look in, right?

PETER. Well, to see how you were. I've got a long-standing engagement with my pupil.

JOANNA. What's the point of your coming around then?

PETER. I thought you liked me to.

JOANNA. Not like this. There's no point to it.

PETER. What will you do this evening?

JOANNA. Don't worry.

PETER. Well, you'll be all right?

JOANNA. Yes, thanks.

PETER. O.K. Well - see you next week perhaps. Right? (*Goes to door, opens it; as he closes it,* cut to:)

Shot of JOANNA, *from his* point of view *sitting as if indifferent on the bed. The door closes on her and* cut to:

28. Interior Hall. PETER, *on the other side of Joanna's door, apprehensively listening. Then turns, walks away, swinging squash bag and brief-case, with an air of release.*

29. Interior. Squash court. PETER *and* SALLUST *playing, PETER running rather flounderingly, his face working, breathing hard, loses the point and rests collapsed against a corner, coughing.*

30. Interior. The changing-room. SALLUST *under a shower,* PETER *sitting on a bench, shaking. Towel around his middle. He has a cigarette, unlit, in his mouth.* SALLUST *emerges.*

PETER. Was that a cold shower?

SALLUST. Mmm.

PETER. Christ!

SALLUST. Well, I go on sweating for hours if I have a hot one. And as I'm taking my girl-friend to the opera -

PETER. Didn't know you liked opera? (*Little pause.*) Didn't know you had a girl-friend, either. Well, I must have assumed you had -

SALLUST. I won't have her for long if I have to keep taking her to the opera. How do you feel?

PETER *grunts.*

You used to be pretty good once, usedn't you? (*Towelling himself vigorously.*) Very nice touch -

PETER. Not really. It's always been cricket for me. Sometimes I still remember a particular shot - I'd never done it before, it was in an under-15 match - it was a late cut. I didn't even know I was going to do it - or was doing it - (*Gets up, demonstrates.*) until I'd completed it - like this - and the ball was at the boundary. The one moment in my life when I felt a touch of sublimity. (*Laughs.*) I try and recall it occasionally, before I go to sleep. (*Begins to dry himself.*)

SALLUST. You know, it just struck me the other day that I was 28 and already too old to be any of the things I still dream I might be - a professional tennis player - or - (*Stands, with a wondering look.*)

PETER. What? (*Turns, looks, smiles.*) Eh?

SALLUST. Actually, a - um (*Vaguely, collapses to the floor.*)

PETER (*runs to him, lifts up his head*). Tommy, Tommy . . . God . . . Tommy.

Two men, carrying squash bags, appear at the end of the dressing-room, come towards PETER, *one of them smoking. Then hurry forward, bend over to look at* SALLUST.

FIRST MAN. Can you do that? Your mouth, kiss him? That business?

PETER *looks at him, then bends over, begins a clumsy kiss of life on* SALLUST.

FIRST MAN. I'll go and get . . . (*Hurries off.*)

PETER (*with* SECOND MAN, *crouching beside him, goes on kissing, draws his mouth away*). I can feel him, he's beginning.

PETER *puts his mouth back over* SALLUST's, *and on his life-kissing, other man beside him, a cigarette between his fingers,* cut to:
FIRST MAN, *standing, scratching meaninglessly at his cheek.*
SECOND MAN *standing beside him, smoking another cigarette. A third man, possibly a doctor, kneels by* SALLUST, *and now wearily straightening.* PETER *observed in the distance, almost obscurely, sitting on the bench, staring blankly ahead and smoking. Various other figures around, including a porter. The* THIRD MAN *gets up, goes over to* PETER, *sits down beside him.*

THIRD MAN. O.K.?

PETER. I felt his breath coming. Out of his mouth.

THIRD MAN. It was probably your own breath coming back at you, I'm afraid.

PETER. He just keeled over. (*Gets up, walks mechanically over to* SALLUST's *body.*)

THIRD MAN. They'll be here in a minute. You look as if you could do with -

PETER *bends down, picks up* SALLUST's *towel, puts it carefully over* SALLUST's *genitals.*

THIRD MAN. I'm sorry.

PETER. He was my pupil, you see. (*Meaninglessly.*)

Stay *on the group as long as possible, then* cut to:

31. Interior. College lecture room. HILARY's *face, seen through the glass-and-wire panels of the door. She is talking, spectacles on, from notes. As she talks, she lifts her head, as if from instinct, looks towards the door, and:*

32. Interior. *From* HILARY's *point of view see* PETER, *on the other side of the glass.*

33. Interior. Charles's study. *They are sitting on the polystyrene sacks, as before. But first,* CHARLES's *voice over, as image maintained from previous scene.*

CHARLES. One of our boys did that - he was 15.

  Cut to *him, pouring a healthy dose of scotch into two glasses.*

  Perfectly fit. Suddenly collapsed on the football pitch. In the midst, so to speak.

PETER (*taking a glass*). Thanks.

  He is by the window, offers CHARLES *a cigarette.* CHARLES *takes it.*

  What is it? (*Turns, looks out of the window.*)

  Cut to:

34. Exterior. Garden. *From* PETER's point of view. CAROLINE *appears, walking slowly.* HILARY *and* CAROLINE *at further end, bent over pram.*

PETER (*voice over*). Half-way upon this way of life I'm lost upon -

CHARLES (*voice over*). Having had 20 years -

  JEREMY *appears, walks after* CAROLINE, *catches up with her. Says something.* CAROLINE *shrugs.*

CHARLES. Having had 20 years, 20 years of *entre deux guerres*, no, that's something else -

  Cut back to:

35. Interior. PETER's *face, turning impassively away from the window.*

CHARLES (*smoking*). The worst is to come, I suppose. The death of friends, all the deaths in waiting, including our own. But it's the death of children that haunts me. Sometimes in the night -

PETER. Don't!

CHARLES (*grunts*). What was he like?

PETER. Just a pupil. Callower than some, in fact I took less notice of him than most of my recent ones until our game - we talked for the first time, you know, the way people do after squash - I patronised him a bit, ignored him quite often, and tried to conceal my irritation when he passed me damned stupid notes in the middle of a plea. He was all right. (*Little pause.*) I don't know.

CHARLES. Everything else all right?

PETER. Mmm?

CHARLES. That girl?

PETER. Oh God, I don't know. I'm keeping it at bay, for the moment.

CHARLES. What?

PETER. Whatever conclusion there's to be. (*Notices* CHARLES's *cigarette.*) Thought you'd given up?

CHARLES. Started again in the hospital waiting-room. (*Inhales deeply, coughs.*)

PETER (*coughs*). Still, that's something to celebrate.

36. Interior. The court. JUDGE *enters, everybody rises, then sits, and as* COUNSEL *for* MR SAWSBURY *rises, the* camera cuts *from face to face, on* MRS SAWSBURY *sitting behind* PETER, *with* ROSE, *to* MR SAWSBURY, *to the* JUDGE, *then* back to MRS SAWSBURY, *tautly apprehensive, then to* PETER *turning, smiles encouragingly,* MRS SAWSBURY *smiles tightly back.* Credits.

	FUNERAL GAMES and THE GOOD AND FAITHFUL SERVANT
	ENTERTAINING MR SLOANE
Harold Pinter	THE BIRTHDAY PARTY
	THE ROOM and THE DUMB WAITER
	THE CARETAKER
	A SLIGHT ACHE and other plays
	THE COLLECTION and THE LOVER
	THE HOMECOMING
	TEA PARTY and other plays
	LANDSCAPE and SILENCE
	OLD TIMES
	NO MAN'S LAND
David Selbourne	THE DAMNED
Jean-Paul Sartre	CRIME PASSIONNEL
Wole Soyinka	MADMEN AND SPECIALISTS
	THE JERO PLAYS
	DEATH AND THE KING'S HORSEMA
Theatre Workshop and Charles Chilton	OH WHAT A LOVELY WAR
Boris Vian	THE EMPIRE BUILDERS
Peter Weiss	TROTSKY IN EXILE
Charles Wood	'H'
	VETERANS
Carl Zuckmayer	THE CAPTAIN OF KÖPENICK

METHUEN PLAYSCRIPTS

Michael Abbensetts	SWEET TALK
Paul Ableman	TESTS
	BLUE COMEDY
Ed Berman/Justin Wintle	THE FUN ART BUS
Barry Bermange	NATHAN AND TABILETH and OLDENBERG
John Bowen	THE CORSICAN BROTHERS
Howard Brenton	REVENGE
	CHRISTIE IN LOVE and OTHER PLAY
	PLAYS FOR PUBLIC PLACES

METHUEN'S THEATRE CLASSICS

METHUEN YOUNG DRAMA

BOLTON OCTAGON THEATRE-IN-EDUCATION COMPANY
Sweetie Pie

BRADFORD ART COLLEGE THEATRE GROUP
John Ford's Cuban Missile Crisis

KEN CAMPBELL
Old King Cole

DAVID CAMPTON
Timesneeze

JOHN CHALLEN
Recreations

DENISE COFFEY
The Incredible Vanishing!!!!

DAVID CREGAN
How We Held the Square

LEEDS THEATRE-IN-EDUCATION COMPANY
Snap Out of It

MITCHELL, LUCIE-SMITH, HUGHES, MARVIN
Playspace

PETER TERSON
The Adventures of Gervase Becket